THE COPERNICAN ERROR:

THE BASIC MISTAKE OF BELIEVING YOU'RE THE CENTER OF EVERYTHING AND SPACE IS COLD AND EMPTY

By

Bruce McCoy

This book is built around
several true stories
about the Kingdom of Heaven.

The Copernican Error
Copyright © by Bruce McCoy

Table of Contents

****

Foreword

Chapter 1 .... The Copernican Error

Chapter 2 .... Good to See You

Chapter 3 .... The Group

Chapter 4 .... The Evidence

Chapter 5 .... Realizing the Kingdom

Chapter 6 .... Lacy's Gift

Chapter 7.. Norson

Chapter 8 .... The Future

FOREWORD

Let's look at life as though it's a road we're traveling. That would be a reasonable analogy. Life is really very much like that. It's like a road (perhaps a railroad) we're moving on. Each day we go a little further.

This is true for each of us as individuals and it's also true for our entire planetary population—all seven billion of us. As we travel down the road, we grow and change. We develop and become more advanced as the natural spiritual beings we truly are. We realize more and more truth as we go. We become wiser.

Also, as we go along the road, we see things differently from different vantage points. When we're at point D or E we can't see certain very important things that we will be able to see when we're at point J or point P. We are "ASLEEP" to these things *now,* but we will wake up to them later when we're further down the road.

It is natural for us to be asleep to important things further down the road. That is an inescapable part of life. For example, we can't see things when we're young that we can see when we're old or we can't see things before we're married that we can see afterward. A *very* good planetary example is that life on this planet is filled with warfare right now. Few of us can see from here that further down the road warfare will stop.

You may be reading this foreword right now as one of those who just can't buy the idea that the *real* universe we live in is populated, organized, and governed by an ancient, unified, wise, totally positive, and truly loving government. If that's how you see it, then perhaps you are also fast asleep to something our entire planet will be waking up to in the not so distant future. Thus, you're operating right now with The Copernican Error at the very foundation of your belief system. The real universe we are living in right now and have been living in since our earliest beginnings is indeed populated, organized, and governed and that is what this book is about.

Chapter One

The Copernican Error

Clack, clack, clack, clackity, clack, clackity, clack, clackity, clack, clack, clack.

Blake (in his private, inner self): I love trains. Time is a train rolling constantly into the future. We're all on it. It's life. We're riding in our little bubble moment on the time train.

It was Wednesday morning at Union Station but not a regular Wednesday. Oh, the huge crowd of daily commuters were there, scurrying all over the big tile floor through the huge expanse of space under the high arched roof. That was as usual, but for Blake it was different. He was headed for New York, not just Baltimore.

He was already in his seat on the Amtrak Special from Washington to New York, and his bulky, full backpack was on the seat beside him. The two seats facing him in his four-seater slot were empty. He was early. He knew that part of the train. He laid his head back and closed his eyes.

The words to an old Southern gospel song were running in a loop in the back of his mind—a song he got from the first album of The Amazing Rhythm Aces years ago: *Life is Like a Mountain Railway*.

Blake (in his private, inner self): It's just astonishing. There ARE the positive secrets of the universe. One is paradox. Maybe we each have a destiny or maybe we're just floating randomly like a feather in the wind. Or, as Forest Gump said, maybe they are both happening at the same time.

Another positive secret is negative to positive transformation. Another is *simplicity*.

It's simply true—we are emotional/spiritual beings. Everything we think, say, or do has an emotional/spiritual background that drives us. It's always either mostly negative or mostly positive. Negative is a source of problems and positive is a source of solutions.

One of the most basic, *simple*, positive secrets, and very important, is that, except for medical problems, *all real human problems are psychological* and *all psychological problems are caused by error.* The errors are usually errors of basic belief and assumption—assumptions about reality. The great bulk of errors stem from one *primary* error—The Copernican Error.

The Copernican Error is the basic mistake of believing that one is the center of *everything* and SPACE is cold, dark, and empty.

The Copernican Error is the error of self-importance or self-centeredness. People are selfish. They have a deep tendency to see themselves and their group or their planet as the center of the universe.

In Copernicus's time the whole of Western society saw itself as the center of reality. They thought the Earth was the center of the cosmos. They thought the Sun circled the Earth. They didn't know the Earth circled the Sun.

Copernicus told them about it and they didn't believe him. For them, the Sun and all the stars existed for the sake of Earth and its "Earthlings." All the movements in the sky were for us. Largely our people still believe that.

Conductor: Hello, Dr. Freeman. It's been a while since I've seen you. (Blake hands him his ticket.)

Blake: Hey, hi, Mr. Souther. It's really good to see you. How're you feeling?

Conductor: Well, I'm still a little slow and tired, but I'm recovering well. I started back to work this past Monday.

Blake: Well, it's really good to have you back. You gave us a bit of a scare there. Are you working full days now?

Conductor: No, I'm just working short days now. I'll be back to full-time week after next.
  I see you're going beyond Baltimore today, huh?

Blake: Yeah, I'm going a little further than usual—all the way to New York.

Conductor: You have some new business?

Blake: Well, I don't know about that. Maybe. I'm going to see a friend. He's got some sort of new and strange things happening. He wanted me to come and see.

Conductor: Well, I'll be with you the whole way. That's my usual trip—Washington to New York and back. I usually do in a day with some time working in New York but on this half-schedule, I'll go straight back and get there just in time to go home from my short day's work. So, if you need anything, just let me know.

Blake: Thanks. It's really good to see you back. I missed you.

Conductor: Yeah, I missed you, too. I missed our talks about The Copernican Error. You know, that idea has really been good for me. I started really seeing myself having the attitude that I have the world at my command as we discussed. I started changing that and it really helped me.

I think Rachel was really glad to see me change like that, too. She used to get really impatient with me, always thinking my way was the only way, and she would do things just to cross me. I excused myself saying kids were just that way. I didn't entertain the idea that maybe I should listen to her some. Then you started talking about The Copernican Error and I started waking up.

Then when I had this heart attack I *really* started realizing I *do not* have the world at my command. Boy!

Blake: Oh Yeah? Well, Souther, I wasn't talking about *you*. You *do* have the world at your command. It's all the rest of us who think we do, but we don't.

Conductor: Aw, don't be saying that stuff now. I tell you what I think. I think it's *you*. You're the one who really has the world at his command and the *rest* of us are fools.

Blake: Oh my! Oh my! Surely *that's* not true. If that's true we're all in *big* trouble.

Conductor: You're *something,* Dr. Freeman. It's really good to see you!
   How are your boys?

Blake: Oh, they're still going a thousand miles an hour . . . and driving me crazy.

Conductor: Well, you know that's what boys are supposed to do.
   Is Robert still beating you at chess?

Blake: Oh yeah, of course *anybody* can beat me at chess. But Robert—I'll never catch Robert!

Conductor: Having met him that one time when he was on the train with you, I have an idea there are a lot of people who'll never catch Robert. He's a pretty impressive fellow.

Blake: Yeah, he is, thanks.

Conductor: Yes, you have every reason to be very proud of that boy. I'm sure Randy is equally as impressive.

Blake: Well, yeah, I guess so—in a *completely* different way.

Conductor: Children are scary, aren't they? Wonderful, but scary.

Blake: I know exactly what you mean.

Conductor: Hey, maybe I'll see you on the way back.

    Mr. Souther walked on to his other customers. Blake lowered the back of his seat and rested his head on the headrest. He closed his eyes, relaxing.

Blake (in his private, inner self): I love seeing the world this way—outside rolling by super-quiet. This big ol' heavy chunk of metal . . . long time to get going, long time to stop, but it rides smooooth. There's that rhythm—steel wheels rolling clack, clack on the track.
    Ahh, relaxation feels good. Lay the back further back . . . there we go.
    What's Evan got going—something about a new business . . . a coffee shop? Pretty wild. I hope I get to go up-town before I leave. I really want to get Lacy something from Saks for her birthday.
    I wonder how they always keep trains smelling this way.

Clackity, clack . . . Clack, clack, clack, clack, clackity, clack, clackity, clack, clack . . .

Blake (in his private, inner self): Hm . . . maybe a nap

Clack, clack, clackity, clack, clackity, clack, clackity, clack . . .

> Oh, Life is like a mountain railway,
> With an engineer so brave.
> We must make the run successful,
> From the cradle to the grave.
> Da da da
>   da da da da da
> Da da da
> Da da da da . . .
>
> Precious Savior, stay beside us,
> 'Til we reach that blissful shore,
> Where the angels wait to join us,
> In God's grace forevermore.
>
> M. E. Abbey, words
Charlie D. Tillman—music

Hm. Off to sleep, for a nice little length of time.

It seemed to Blake, as he was dozing, that someone sat down on the seat facing him.

Blake (in his private, inner self): Curious. As I recall, there were plenty of empty seats in this car. I'll just be real still; he'll think I'm sleeping.

Hm, wonder if we're out of the city into the country yet . . . Oh yeah . . . there it is, Norman Rockwell America with motion, no sound . . . not so much the fast-moving motion here in the foreground going the other way, but the slower stuff back there further away—cars moving on that country road, Canadian geese flying over the field in their raggedy V, completely silent.

Stranger: Hello, are you awake?

Blake (pausing for a look to see who's talking to him): Yeah, I guess I am.

Stranger: I couldn't tell if you were awake or not. You were very still and your eyes were closed but your face had a slight expression, your mouth was closed and your breathing didn't seem like that of someone sleeping.

Blake: You sound like a real student of whether or not someone is awake.

Stranger: Interestingly, that sort of ties in with why I sat down here. You may be wondering. I hope you don't mind, but I saw the title of that little book you have on your lap, *The War Against Sleep* by Colin Wilson.

Blake (in his private, inner self): I ought to wake up pretty good right here. I don't need to shut him out, even though I am grumpy about being disturbed. He's not really doing anything bad. Blake, watch yourself. Don't let your negativity drive you.

Blake: Are you familiar with the work of Gurdjieff and Ouspensky?

Stranger: I *am* and I've read that book. Wilson's a good writer. Gurdjieff basically says life is about waking up. Right?

Blake: Right. *People are asleep,* and not asleep as in the bed at night.

Stranger: Right. People are asleep when they are going through their regular daily life.

Blake: A major thing about people is that they have an intractable tendency to be unaware of important things. They are ASLEEP to these important things. Being asleep is a form of denial—denial of very important *basic* truth. Literally everyone does it.

Stranger: They are asleep to what's *really* going on in the unseen facts and forces of their lives, underneath the surface.

Blake: Yes, people are asleep during what they think of as their waking hours. They *think* they are awake, and they *are* a little bit, but in *very* important ways they are generally *very* asleep. They are particularly asleep to their deep, basic ego motivations. I call this their Copernican Error. This is the *bottom line* level of their motivation where they see everything as revolving around them. It's their basic sense of self-importance—their fundamental selfishness.

People's motivations are usually mixed. They may be *aware* of wanting to help someone or do something good but *underneath* that, they want to boost their ego or very selfishly get recognition or some kind of social power.

When you point it out to them and say, "You're being motivated by your ego or your Copernican Error," they say, "No, I'm not." They say they're being motivated for the good of society or to help someone, and they might be, but, underneath, they're also motivated by their ego. There are many different actions and situations where this kind of situation obtains.

Stranger: What are some of the more specific, important ways this sleepiness can be seen?

Blake (in his private, inner self): Who is this guy? How interesting to run into him right now.

Blake (aloud): People are asleep to the unknown and they're asleep to uncertainty. They're asleep to their errors of assumption. They're asleep to the here and now. They're asleep to eternalness. They're asleep to who they are. They're asleep to what life's about and what's really going on. They're asleep to positivity and true love. They're asleep to the negativity that blocks their spiritual development. They're asleep to the future. They're asleep to the schemes their minds come up with and the fact that their minds lie to them constantly. They're asleep to the cigarette butts they threw down and the fact that they're still there. They're asleep to the unseen and they're asleep to being asleep. They're asleep to the big picture and the little picture and the fact that the outer material world is permeated by illusion.

People are often asleep to whether they feel negative or positive toward someone, let's say, someone they're talking to. Are they trying to beat that person or cooperate with them? They are asleep to whether they are afraid in a situation or whether they are angry or loving. They're often asleep when they are motivated to look good to others. They're asleep to the fact that they are doing something out of their jealousy or a desire to win or a desire to manipulate events or get someone else to do what they want.

Stranger: What's an example of that?

Blake: The most outstanding example is when people are arguing. Most everyone argues from time to time. Many argue a lot. When they're arguing, their attention is focused on their *point*. They're thinking about the point they're trying to make on their side of the argument. They think that's what they're doing. But *it's not*. What they're doing is power struggling. They are wrangling with their opponent for power—who's going to win, who's going to be up, who's going to have the most power or respect? They usually operate under the illusion that if they argue well enough they will actually *win*, but they're asleep to this illusion. They are entirely asleep to what's *really* going on. What's really going on is a *power struggle* that *no one* is going to win.

Stranger: That's a really good example. It's so good because *everybody* does it.

Blake: Every person tends to be asleep to the mutual impact that each has on the other. People are asleep to the intense rivalry they feel toward others at work, and they're asleep to the things there are about this person that make him or her likeable and deserving of care. People are asleep to the fact that they're just making excuses when they blame someone else for a problem. They're asleep to the thing they've been ignoring that pops up and bites them in the butt. They're asleep to the thing in their unconscious that's going to work against them or hurt them all of a sudden.

    They are asleep to the fact that the thing they hate about someone else is really something they do themselves that they don't like and want to deny. They're asleep about how much time they spend being negative. They're asleep to the fact that someone else's obnoxious behavior is a plea for help. They're asleep to what will *really* make them happy and how to get it. They're asleep to the fact that they're being tricked by their mind into doing or thinking something is true but it isn't true or important. They tend to be asleep to many very important things—things that are major keys to growth and better living.

Stranger: Boy, that's a *lot* of ways people are asleep.

Blake: Waking up to these things expands and strengthens your inner spiritual self. It is true spiritual growth, and it is what life is really about. It is good to wake up to what motivates us. Our emotional values and reactions, down in the back of our mind, drive us. They make us think about how we think and feel, and how we feel and do what we do. If we're awake to them we can work with them, correct them, and make them better.

Stranger: What about God? Do you think people are asleep to God?

Blake: Yes, people tend to forget about God or create their own notions about God that work for them but allow them to keep hiding or being asleep to things they don't want to wake up to. For example, God wants them to be compassionate and to serve others.

Stranger: Are you saying people *want* to be asleep to things?

Blake: Yes. That's a *big* reason people are asleep. It's not the *only* reason but it's *big*. People are asleep to many things because they want to be and they're usually asleep to the fact that they want to be asleep. It's the error that comes from the mother of *all* errors—The Copernican Error. They are full of self-importance. They are self-centered.

People stay asleep because they don't want to give up their negativity or their self-importance. People are asleep to the fact that other people are like them and they don't *want* that to be true. They want to be different and better than other people. Our Copernican Error makes us *need* to be *better* than they. So we tend to be asleep to the fact that the other person has a family and a history and loved ones and problems and wise insights and a need to be loved.

Stranger: Right. I can see that.

Blake: People tend to be asleep to the fact that other people have full lives just like they do. This is basic self-centeredness. The other person is not just someone to beat or to be better than or whose life has nothing important going on, but that's how we want to see him or her. People are fundamentally negative and competitive with other people, and we tend to be asleep to this negativity and competition. Transforming negative to positive is one of the positive secrets.

Being negative is about relating to others by way of comparisons and competing with them—"compared to you, I'm better/you're worse." This gives us an easy way of defining who we are. We are a person who is better than those other persons. It's easy and we don't want to wake up to the fact that it's negative and a source of trouble . . . and not *really* accurate.

We don't want to wake up to the fact that we'd rather be against others and in competition with them than to be positively *with* them, cooperating and loving. When we stay negative toward others, we keep them at arm's length so we won't have to go through all the emotional risk and upheaval of caring for them and helping them.

This is easier and more satisfying to our negative self. Even though we're not aware of it, we *do know* that the positive way is better in the long run and we *do* choose it to some extent.

Stranger: We want to keep our superior position because we're thinking the way our negative orientation makes us think.

Blake: People are asleep to important things, particularly their selfishness. They're also asleep to the fact that they're asleep. This makes it doubly difficult to wake up. So they're *really* asleep to the extent that it's almost impossible to wake up.

They can't overcome this until they *see* how important waking up is, and they actually become positive about doing it. Waking up is a positive thing but it takes much more work, awareness, and creativity than negativity does.

Stranger: It's good to wake up to waking up and it's also good to wake up to being positive.

Blake: That's right. It's impressive that you see that.

Stranger: It's pretty interesting. This is new stuff for me.

There was a short silence.

Blake (in his private, inner self): This guy is rather bright. He just told me he's having a realization. Maybe I should slow down a bit and give him a little time to reflect.

Blake: Another important way most people are asleep is that they miss or ignore the fact that life is not *really* very much about the outer, physical world. The outer, physical world is perfect for materialistic indulgence. It feeds our Copernican Error desires. But just because we can see something or hear it doesn't mean it's the main thing. But it's easy to think that.

The most important things in life are imperceptible with our five physical senses. It's not about what you achieve or get or have to brag about in the outer physical world. It's also not about how nice your house is or your car or any of your material assets.

Life is about the growth and development of the inner, spiritual self. Life is about waking up. People are asleep to what life is really about and the importance of waking up to it. They need to wake up to waking up.

Stranger: Are you a psychologist?

Blake: Yes.

Stranger: What kind of psychologist are you?

Blake: I'm a professional psychotherapist.

Blake (in his private, inner self): Is *he* a psychologist? Since everyone is, I guess he is. He's a pretty good one in ways. I think I won't ask him. Let it be a mystery.

Stranger: What is the most important thing you would say about psychotherapy and how it works?

Blake: Psychotherapy is about spiritual development. The key is learning how to wake up and see the important things we're asleep to. The self-important and selfish desires that underlie what we do create erroneous assumptions and priorities. When we wake up, we can learn to correct these errors.

Stranger: That's so right and so simple. You're saying both the negative to positive transformation and basic simplicity are positive secrets of the universe.

Blake: Yes. It's great that you have heard me on those points. You've heard me so well that you're saying them back to me. That is psychotherapy. It's about the process of realization—seeing the positive secrets of the universe. The positive secrets are gems of wisdom to wake up to and *realize*. When you see them clearly enough and realize them enough to use them you can begin to transform your negatives to positives. *that* is psychotherapy.

Everybody practices psychotherapy without knowing it. It's natural. It's a normal life function like walking, making friends, and thinking about things. We all live in a psychological world. We learn about psychology and we try to use it to help ourselves. That's psychotherapy, but we generally don't do it very well. Psychotherapy is about changing negative to positive and correcting error. We don't see that very well.

Stranger: Correcting error and changing negative to positive.

Blake: Yes, we're usually in error about life and what's *really* going on. These erroneous assumptions are down inside in our inner spiritual self—our deep, unconscious mind. Most people are *very much* in error about how we *really are* and how it would be best for us to be. Generally, down in the deep mind we have a lot of negativity and we don't need it. Our negativity is very erroneous. We are asleep to these errors.

Stranger: So we have to wake up to see the errors that create our problems.

Blake: Right. We need to have *therapeutic* realizations.

Stranger: And the *most basic* error is The Copernican Error.

Blake: Yes—*The Copernican Error.* It's the error of *self-centeredness* or *ego*. We see everything in terms of an underlying desire or need to *serve ourselves* and be at the center of everything—to have the world at our command.

Stranger: Yes! I *see* that! The people in Copernicus's time thought the Earth, *their Earth*, was the center of everything. They thought the Earth stood still and the Sun moved across the sky. This theory of how the solar system worked was based on natural self-centeredness, Earth-centeredness.

Blake: And not only does The Copernican Error distort the judgment of all of us today on personal and socio-cultural levels, it also distorts our view of the workings of the *universe,* just as it did in the days of Copernicus.

Today we think space is cold, dark, and empty except for physical objects like stars and planets. Despite what reason would tell us and the fast-mounting evidence that there are other inhabited planets, we think *we* are the only beings living in space.

Stranger: We don't see that The Copernican Error is as big for us as it was for the people in Copernicus's time, do we? We don't see the similarity between people now and those in Copernicus's time. We're asleep to this.

Blake: Right. We don't see that we *want* or *need* space to *not* have people in it. We *need* to be the main ones. All of us have a natural tendency to see everything in life as centered around ourselves. It's a very powerful and effective force when it comes to raw, basic survival, but it's a problem when it dominates our view of everything and makes us unable to see things that are very true but have nothing to do with protecting or serving *"me."* The Copernican Error *does* tend to dominate us this way.

Stranger: I remember when I was very young, I first had the realization that the major problems in life come from selfishness. It was a *major* realization for me and has been ever since. All my life I have continued to affirm and reaffirm this basic realization. I believe even more now that by far our biggest source of problem is selfishness.

Blake: You can see how appropriate it is to call it The Copernican Error. It shows how *basic* the ego error is. Along with all the other self-centered things we do; the people of Earth *still* function with the same kind of error about the universe that was there in Copernicus's time. We think it's all about us. We think we're the main show. We're not aware. We're asleep to how things really are in the heavens.

    The *real* fact is that the universe we live in, that's right there in that sky, is hugely populated with many different orders of beings. They are organized and governed by one ancient, established government.

Stranger: Wait a minute now. You're not just saying space is populated *a little*, you're saying it is *fully* populated and it is organized into a central government that governs the whole thing. And I suppose you're saying the universe government, unlike ours, does a *very good job*.

Blake: Right. Absolutely! The universe's government works wonderfully. And it is actually *our* government. We will gradually see this more and more. As a planetary population, we will realize what's *really true*; it will become our formally established government.

Stranger: That's going a little bit too far for me.

Blake: Yes, that's not surprising. It's very natural, too. Of course you have doubt. "Our people don't believe in such things!" You believe that *maybe* there are other inhabited planets out there but you don't want to believe there are very many and you don't want to believe that they are more intelligent than we or that their government should rule us. Can you see this as The Copernican Error operating in you?

Stranger: Let's say I can see how *you* would see it that way. I can't exactly see my opinion as based in The Copernican Error right now. I don't think there is any evidence that the universe is quite so *advanced* in its development as you are saying it is.

    There was a short silence. The stranger just sat and looked at Blake for a short while that seemed not so short. Finally he said,

Stranger: How did you get so certain about all of this?"

Blake: Well, you know, we all follow a different course in life. I've never been one to accept conventional beliefs without examining them thoroughly. I've been studying things like these a long time—things such as psychology, the unconscious, cosmology, theology, philosophy, and the universe and its possibilities. There really is quite a bit of evidence to support what I've said to you. To me it is completely convincing.

Stranger: What is the evidence?

Blake: Right now, I don't think my reciting a lot of evidence is what's going to help the most. Instead, let's look at where you are.
    First, you understand the whole idea of being asleep and you agree with it. Second, you are fairly accepting of the idea that there are other beings or "aliens" living on other planets. You just have problems with the idea that the universe is so *full* of beings of all levels of intelligence and a *very good* and effective government is governing them all, even though you know we've been told about this.

Stranger: Wait. You say we have been told about it. When were we told about it?

Blake: Well, for one thing Jesus told us about it. We just don't think the "Kingdom of Heaven" He was talking about is the same one I'm talking about.

Stranger: But to you it is.

Blake: Yes.

Stranger: So, what do you suggest I do, or what should *we* do?

Blake: If we say you're asleep to the kind of universe I'm talking about then the question becomes, why do you resist waking up about it? It's either true or not true. If it's *not* true then you're right and you should resist. If it *is* true then, the question is why do you *want* the true thing to be untrue?

Stranger: Right, and I *really* can't see that it's true. I really don't believe it's possible. I figure if it were true, we would know about it. You think I'm being arrogant and exaggerating the real truth-knowing abilities of Earth culture, don't you?

Blake: Have you ever been hypnotized?

Stranger: No, never. I don't know much about hypnotism.

Blake: Maybe an experience with hypnotism would help you see a little bit more into your conflict

Stranger: Do you think so? Sounds rather interesting. Are you offering to hypnotize me? How long are we talking about?

Blake: Yes, I can do it. It'll take about a half an hour or forty-five minutes. I believe you will find it helpful and enjoyable. Nothing will happen that's not okay with you and you will remember everything when it's over. All hypnosis is self-hypnosis so it will really be you doing it. I'll just provide leadership and structure.

Stranger: Okay, let's try it.

Blake: Okay, the way we start is to sit straight and comfortable with your head and your whole body relaxed. Don't cross your legs or arms, and listen to my voice.

Blake was speaking now in a slow, musical, resonant voice that was very peaceful and pleasant.

Blake: First you relax your feet and ankles, then your calves, then your thighs, your lower abdomen, lower back and so on up your body. I will lead you by giving you phrases that you will repeat to yourself (pause). Here we go (pause).

Stranger: Okay.

Blake: Let's start by paying attention to the clacking of the wheels of the train on the track. You can hear the Clacking—clack, clack, clack, clack. There it is, in rhythm: Clack, clack, clack (pause).

Whatever you do, keep noticing and paying attention to the rhythm of the train. Now it is time to begin to move in the direction of a trance. The muscles of your feet and ankles are feeling relaxed. Your feet and ankles are feeling heavy and warm. And the muscles of your calves are relaxing. The muscles of your calves are feeling warm and open. The muscles of your thighs are feeling relaxed. The muscles of your thighs are feeling warm and heavy. You are listening to the clack clack rhythm of the train.

For the next few minutes Blake continued to give the stranger phrases with which he told himself to relax various muscle groups of his body moving up through his trunk, shoulders, neck, face, and head. He also led him into taking deep cleansing breaths and continuing to pay attention to the rhythm of the train.

Blake: Your muscles are relaxing more and more. You take a deep breath drawing the air all the way down to the bottom of your stomach and easily exhaling again. Take another deep breath as we listen to the clack, clack of the wheels of the train.

We are moving now in the direction of a relaxed hypnotic trance as we listen to the clacking of the wheels.

Yes, that's right. Your eyes are heavy and closed as you continue to relax and listen with more and more focus on the clacking of the wheels. We will continue to relax while at the same time pay attention to the clacking of the train wheels. You can hear that very well, right?

The stranger nodded.

Blake: The wheels are steady in beating out a rhythm. As we go, we become more and more relaxed. The more relaxed we become the deeper we go into a trance. The train is carrying us deeper and deeper and deeper as we go further down the track into a relaxed trance.

Blake's voice was a part of the train now and the stranger was showing signs of entering a deep hypnotic trance. His breathing was deep, slow, and regular. His heart rate also appeared a bit slower and very steady. Blake continued to talk with him in a way that now seemed very familiar and a part of the experience for him.
He was very relaxed. His breathing and his pulse rate was very steady, strong, and slow. It was time to try a test to see him follow suggestions and have a powerful enough experience to be meaningful.

Blake: You know now that you have embarked upon a very exciting and fulfilling journey. The train is carrying you to a place that you know is very safe and pleasant for you. It is a place you've been expecting for a long time and you know new and interesting things are about to happen. They are things you want and have been looking forward to. As you think about these things, your hand begins to rise up into the air above your head and make a go-ahead movement with your fist because you are very pleased about what is happening.

As he was saying this, the stranger's right hand began to move up off his lap and into the air over his head. He moved it around and gave a circular go-ahead movement with his fist indicating enthusiasm for what was happening. His hand came back down to his lap.

Blake: You are creating a picture of the place you are going in your mind. It is a place of peace and solitude. You will not meet with anyone there. You will meet only with yourself just as you are meeting with yourself right now. You will have a very interesting conversation with new ideas that are quite stimulating. You have not entertained these ideas before and yet they seem very obvious. The train continues to carry you, clack, clack, clack, toward this destination place that you picture in your mind. Can you see it?

There was a pause for a couple of moments and then the stranger spoke in a measured way very typical of someone in a deep trance.

He said softly,

Stranger: "Yes, I can see it."

Blake: How do you like it?

Stranger: I like it very much. It makes me very happy.

Blake: You are continuing to ride this train along with my voice and we have entered a deep trance. We know where we're going and though we've never been here before, we know the whole journey is safe and positive.

We will continue on the journey until it comes to its end and we have experienced what there is here for us. When we do come to the end, I will say we are coming to the end and I will count to five and say, "It is time now to end our journey and return to normal conditions." Then I will clap my hands and at that time you can come back to the normal conditions we were in. You will be able to clearly remember in vivid detail everything that happened during the journey. Until then let's continue our journey.

The train you are riding is familiar to you. You ride these trains all the time but today you are riding it alone. You may have different things you would like to do while we're riding. You may open your eyes and look out the window or you may get up and go get a drink of water but you will not see any living thing inside the train. You will see no other people in the car we're riding. The car is empty. You are the only one here.

After only a couple of seconds, the stranger began to move in his seat. At first he squirmed a little, pulled up his feet, and leaned forward lifting his elbows in a kind of stretching motion. He opened his eyes and leaned over toward the window (he was sitting in a seat beside the aisle). He peered out the window for a few seconds saying nothing and looking very much like a man who was alone. Then he turned back toward the aisle and looked both ways up and down the aisle. No one was moving through the aisle at that time, so that was not something he had to deal with. The train had been traveling through the countryside for quite some time and the passengers were very settled in. Some were sleeping, others were reading; things were very quiet.

The stranger stood up in front of his seat, still looking like a man alone. Then, without looking the other way, he moved out into the aisle and began making his way toward the end of the car that was nearest. He moved along the aisle touching the tops of the backs of the seats as many people would.

He came to the end of the car where there was a water fountain. He bent down to the fountain and got a long drink of water and straightened up again, swaying and swinging his arms a bit as though he felt very relaxed. Then he began moving back along the aisle toward his seat. Blake was sitting diagonally across from him.

At this time there was a man moving toward him in the aisle. When the man got somewhat close, he moved into an open seat, bent down to peer out the window, and stood up again to move back out into the aisle after the man had gone by. Blake was spellbound watching all of this. The stranger came back to his seat and sat down completely ignoring Blake.

Blake: How has your journey been so far?

The stranger responded to Blake's question but he did not look Blake's way.

Stranger: It's been really terrific for me. I really like this place I've come to. It's beautiful. I don't know if I've ever enjoyed being by myself quite this much. I've also really enjoyed having my own train to ride in. I really like riding in trains.

Blake: I like train rides, too, and this one has been a good one. Now we're coming to the end. It is time now to end our journey and return to normal conditions.

After about a second, Blake clapped his hands and watched the stranger to see his response. The stranger batted his eyes a little and looked around. He saw the train car and the people sitting in the seats. Then he looked at Blake and a big smile came slowly over his face.

Blake: What was it like?

Stranger: Wow! It was quite an experience. I loved the train ride and going to that great place in the garden where I was alone (pause). But the main thing was the empty train. I got up and walked over to get some water and the entire car was completely empty. There were *no* people and I thought that was just fine. I thought that was how it really was.

 I think your idea for this hypnotic experience was very ingenious. I don't really know how it works but I do find myself much more ready to entertain the idea that maybe space is not quite as empty as I was believing and it could actually be organized and governed in a far more ideal and positive way than I assumed. If I ask myself the question, "What is the probability that space is organized and civilized far more than we are?" I would say my estimate of the probability has increased quite a bit because of the hypnotic experience. I *really* believed that the train car was empty, when I actually *knew* it wasn't. It makes me very aware now that people are asleep to things and people deny things. And it's true of *me*, not just everybody else.

Blake: Much as I've seen it happen, I never cease to be amazed by therapeutic realizations and how they work. I have to say I don't *really* know exactly how they work. But they *do* happen and they *do* change people. And they *really* are quite common. Everyone has them on a regular basis, at least small ones.

Stranger: They seem to kind of help people move along. That's what I feel happened to me.

Blake: Yes, they help people move along down in the deep unconscious mind where what we believe about reality seems to be organized and where our motivations come from.

Stranger: Yes, I think I never realized quite so clearly how much our opinions about reality and our beliefs about what's true are connected to what you call our deep mind. I also understand that you are saying the *deep* mind is the same thing as the unconscious mind.

Blake: Yes, that's right. I think so. I notice you're talking about realizations and I really like that. Realizations are exactly the kind of learning experiences I think are needed in these kinds of situations.

Stranger: I have to say, I would still like to hear the evidence you mentioned. I think I'm a lot more open to giving it a more honest consideration after my, uh, hypnotic train ride.

Blake: There is really quite a lot of evidence. For one thing we've seen just in the last twenty years or so a tremendous increase in the number of planets being found by our astronomers.

First, they figured a technique for finding planets and then they figured more techniques and got better and better at it. Now they find them all the time.

Then there's the whole UFO citation thing and the pretty credible rumors about our government having exchanges with aliens.

Then there is just the generally fast movement of the opinions of "the man on the street." When I was young, if you asked the man on the street if there were other inhabited planets the response would *always* be a resounding *no*. But these days most people would say yes.

There is also this fact that I'm aware of and most people aren't that the highest rulers of the universe government have sent us a book that tells about the entire universe civilization in considerable detail.

Stranger: *Really?*

Blake: Yes.

Stranger: What's the name of it and why haven't I heard of it?

Blake: Well, I suppose you haven't heard of it because of what we were talking about a little while ago—people are asleep. Not very many people are aware of the Book. People don't seem to *want* to know about it. It "hides in plain view" so to speak. It's available, though. You can get it.

Stranger: What's its title?

Blake pulls out his wallet and takes out a personal business card. He writes the name of the book on the back of the card and offers it to the stranger.

Just at that moment the stranger looked out the window and he realized that the train had stopped at his station. He didn't know how long they'd been sitting there and he panicked. He felt the train do a very slight little jerk just when it started to move again.

Stranger: Oh my! This is my stop and we're starting to move again. *I have to go!* Sorry to leave you so abruptly but I have to get off before they won't let me off. Bye! Thanks *very* much. It was a fascinating experience.

At that point the stranger looked briefly at Blake. He grabbed the card Blake held in his hand and rushed off down the aisle, leaving Blake as unceremoniously as he had come.

Blake watched the stranger hurry down the aisle to exit the train. It had been an interesting encounter. He was a little sorry to see him go, especially so abruptly, but he was not sad to be left again to his private thoughts.

Blake (in his private, inner self): Wow, there he goes and I didn't even get his name. At first I didn't want to know his name. I was grumpy about his bursting in on me. But now I like him. I guess during the course of our exchange I could see he's a very interesting guy. He's a great example of how hard it is for regular Americans to see the truth about the Universe Kingdom. I have to learn to be patient. I have a hard time being satisfied to go at an evolutionary pace. I think about how great it will be when it is common and accepted knowledge that we live in Jesus' "Kingdom of Heaven," and I easily forget how long it's going to take and all the argument and struggle that will be involved before the majority of people really see that it's true. It is really true what they say in the field of psychotherapy, "People choose known hells and reject unknown heavens." People *really* do that.

He continued to think about a lot of the meanings and implications of the subject matter that he and the stranger had covered. He wondered if the stranger would look seriously at the book he had told him about. It was a real toss up from his point of view as to whether the stranger would go enough out of his way to actually look up the book and read enough to see what it is. People are all very different and it's next to impossible to know which of the various ones of them will be interested enough to actually wake up and see the truth about our cosmic context.

Before long he drifted off to sleep again and slept quite well until Mr. Souther gently shook him, saying that they had arrived in New York and it was time to disembark. He got up from his seat, grabbed his backpack, and walked out of the train onto one of the platforms in Grand Central Station.

He made his way to the main part of the station and found the gate that led him down into the subway tunnels where the trains would come and take him to the Lower East Side.

Chapter Two

Good to See You

Blake felt a slight but noticeable WHOOOSH of expansion as he came up the final steps from the subway tunnels. There's a hint of possible adventure as he stepped out into the pulsing city. A hint can mean a lot. No telling what's going on with his old friend Evan with whom he will be meeting. Something interesting is up from what Evan said on the phone.

He felt a muted excitement. He moved slowly on the sidewalk trying to get his bearings. He had to find the new coffee house where Evan wants to meet. He noticed iron railings on stoops, iron covers here and there, old rusty grates, pieces of sandwich wrappers and newspapers, plastic bags, long melted pieces of candy and fallen gum wads, and ancient cigarette butts copper colored along with the unidentifiables.

There were closed windows with walls of curtains/drapes; others have clear glass that let you see inside a little. Some windows were partially open. His subliminal awareness felt the close canyon-like narrow streets lined with seven- to ten-story brick and brownstone buildings. Traces of bikes were chained to railings and iron lamp posts, garbage cans stood in the corner where the stoops and buildings met, trying to be invisible but not making it. All these things floated in the sleepy wings of his mind.

A man in a beautifully tailored suit with expensive shirt, a big collar, and no tie was talking to a ruddy, smaller man in old worn patchy jeans, a greasy jacket, long unruly dreads, and bright twinkly eyes. Their conversation was relaxed but focused. Now and again they laughed or looked down and said nothing. Two women walked down the street hand in hand. Two men walk down the street hand in hand. Two dogs walked down the street running interference, their masters well in hand. It's every street of every big city in the world but the peculiarly intense and concentrated version that is the Lower East Side of Manhattan. It's the ocean of humanity that is New York City.

Blake was all of a sudden immersed. It's like every city and no other city. He wondered how many cities like New York City there are across the entire universe of universes—each one having its Earth-like little planet. "Probably more than there are total cities on Earth," he thought to himself. "How do they differ? How are they the same? Some of them must know as little about us as we do about them but probably not many."

Blake (in his private, inner self): Think of all those cities across the universe. I'm here right now in this one. There are trillions of us—people like me and we all have this little fragment of you, Heavenly Father. We have you just like I have you right now but I *don't know it* for certain. I only know it—I only know you—by faith and by long-time familiarity. I *really* believe it and have for a very long time. So I'm certain it's true but yet, *paradoxically*, I don't know you at all. I'm *alone* as I know you want me to be so I can be *completely* free, *truly* completely free so that I can truly *choose* you, love you, and bring myself to you with a *high quality* of awareness and intention.

Here go the bobbing pigeons and scruffy little sparrows, pecking at random things visible and invisible. There were horns honking, motors sounding uuddn-uuddn'n, gears grinding, wheels humming, people hollering far away. They melded into a general din and clatter to the beat of heels, variously fashionable, clicking on the pavement—people flowing, coming and going, constantly, persistently.

One could smell the roasting chestnuts, warm pretzels, and franks. One could also feel the long-time "smell" of humanity mixed with everything—sweat, steel, money, concrete, poverty, error, effort, dreams, depression, urine, illusion, whiskey, greed, and wine. People were everywhere—some milling around, others reading, maybe talking, all watching, talking to themselves, maybe lost or found: no telling where.

Something Blake hasn't noticed, but he would say yes if you asked, is that there were two kinds of people on the street—those who look you in the eye and those who don't. In the constant shuffle, people were going through their lives, all aware of one another. Some acknowledged Blake by looking at him while others ignored him by not catching his eye, as if they were pretending he was not there.

Blake noticed things but he was not holding them in his awareness—they just passed through. His attention was elsewhere. He was thinking about seeing Evan again, anticipating the experience. He and his old friend were going to share some "new coffee." He thought he knew what this meant. Evan used the term and, knowing Evan, Blake figured it's some trendy new drink. It would be very enjoyable, maybe even sensational, but he had no idea about the real truth. It was beyond his wildest imagination. He could never predict it was something that would change his life.

He knew he was not someone who always keeps his ear to the ground, so he was not surprised that Evan knew about it before he did. But now he knew and that was good enough. He isn't adept at keeping up with new things, but he felt pretty good about having friends like Evan who could fill him in.

He was looking forward to seeing Evan. They hadn't seen each other in quite a while. They live in different cities. Each has his own life and family. These days they don't think a lot about each other for long periods of time. Their friendship goes back to their days in graduate school when the whole world was a huge interlocking potpourri of drama and intrigue.

At that time they forged a special relationship, the kind that lasts, and though they may go for long periods with no contact, they understand each other and their commitment never fades. They always know they can catch up with each other at any time.

Their friendship is important to each of them. It's made to be long lasting. They are that kind of people—the kind who form strong friendships and maintain commitments throughout long periods. When they meet there won't be a lot of time spent trying to "catch up" about the past. They'll just jump right into the present and start talking about what's going on.

Blake (in his private, inner self): Well, I know Evan. What an interesting mixture of wild, whimsical, flamboyance and tight "gotta get it right" businessman. I know I have my doubts as to the real value of this "New Coffee" but he's my friend, my long time *old* friend. I'll get to see him again, and Jennifer, and their little girl, Claire. I've never seen her before except in pictures. It'll be good to see them all. From everything they've said in Christmas letters, phone calls, e-mails, and such it seems as though they're doing well.

The Starlight café and Coffee Shop was a new business venture for Evan. He said on the phone that he was sure it would be a roaring success. Soon everyone would be talking about Starlight Coffee Houses and the new coffee. Blake was taking that with a grain of salt. Evan has always been given to exaggeration and hyperbole; but Blake is still quite curious about what has Evan so worked up. It seemed he was more excited than usual, even for Evan.

Blake (to a little guy with a big moustache standing on the corner under the Essex Street sign): Which way is Christie Street?

Little Guy: That way (as he pointed with the forefinger of his left hand). What's over there? Why are you going over there?

Blake: I'm going to a little place right next to the Bowery Ballroom (looking over in the direction he's pointing).

Little Guy: Ahh, the new coffee shop (he looked at Blake with renewed interest).

Blake: You've heard of it.

Little guy: Yeah, go on over there. You'll like it.

    A big smile came over the man's face. He smiled and looked at Blake right in the eye. Blake smiled back, impressed that he knew and liked Evan's coffee shop.

Blake: You've been there?

Little Guy: Oh yeah. It's a great little place. They put magic in your coffee.

Blake: They do? Uh, well isn't that something . . .

    Blake pulled away from the man's engaging gaze and began to move up Delancey Street. It was only three or four blocks to the Bowery Ballroom. Blake hiked his backpack up a little tighter and started walking.
    The man at the booth selling magazines, papers, and candy was looking at him hoping to sell him something. Two drunk street guys were talking "a lot a jive." Several attractive women dressed in tight jeans and nice fitting

dresses passed through his view. He watched them in that way where no one sees he's watching.

He couldn't tell how long the few blocks take, but he covered them easily. Memory impressions of past trips to the city were coming alive in the back of his mind—people arguing, people selling, people singing, a crazy man throwing a rabbit around on the sidewalk. He remembered again the sense of thousands of people packed into this beehive of concrete and steel all living their private lives as though they're the only ones there. He remembered the steamy smell of the street with its hint of all smells mixed together.

Soon he was there, looking at the marquee above the six doors of the Bowery Ballroom. Next door, a sign was across the windows of the little shop and read: The Starlight Cafe and Coffee Shop, Home of The New Coffee. Quite a few customers were sitting and milling around inside. A group of three people were entering at the door. He followed them in.

The shop was brightly lit and colorful inside with logo type pictures of cups of coffee and delicious eats on the walls along with a menu offering pastries, other baked goods, and some sandwiches such as chicken salad, egg salad, corned beef, hotdogs, and bagels with cream cheese. There were a couple of signs that say, "Try the Coffee With the Drops. It Helps You Think" and "Try the Coffee With Magic In It."

As Blake walked in, he saw Evan behind the counter tending to some customers. Evan saw Blake and waved. Then he held up one finger indicating he would be right there. As soon as he was finished with the customers, he looked at Blake and their eyes connected.

Evan: Hey, man. It's great to see you!

He walked over to greet Blake and hugged him in the middle of the shop. They're both smiling wide.

Blake: Hey, Evan, here you are again in the middle of thick city.

Evan: How was your trip? Did you have any trouble finding us?

Blake: No, I asked a man right after I came up from the subway and he seemed to know this place well, says he's been here and says you "put magic" in the coffee. He seemed to like it a lot.

Evan called to a waitress named Stacy and gestured for her to meet them at an empty table against the wall. They moved there and sat down across from one another.

Blake: What's so special about this coffee?

Evan: Let's see if you can tell. You were a major character for me when I first experienced it.

Blake: Me? How's that? What did I do? When did that happen?

Evan: You talked about the universe being fully populated, organized, and governed. You were totally convinced it's true.

Blake: Oh yeah? It *is* true!

Stacy had come with two mugs and a pot of coffee. She put the mugs down on coasters in front of each of the two friends and filled them. Then she took a plastic bottle from a holder on her apron and, using a dropper, she put two drops of a clear liquid in their mugs of coffee.

Blake: What's that stuff? Is that the "magic" she's putting in the coffee?

Evan: Sort of.

Blake: Is it some kind of drug? What are you running here, an opium den?"

Evan (laughing): Yeah, that's it—a new kind of opium den. Drink up (holding his mug up high in the air) and nod off into oblivion!

Blake: So I figure into this thing because of what I know about the universe.

Blake half mumbles this, maybe mostly to himself. This was a surprising twist for Blake—something he hadn't considered.

Somehow, years after he first made his comment about the universe being organized, Evan woke up to the truth of what he had said. It was a long time ago because he hadn't seen Evan in years. Nevertheless Blake's interest in the whole thing was now quite intensified—more personal.

Evan (looking at him intently): I don't suppose you remember the last time we were together.

Blake had a blank look. He shrugged.

Evan: I was in Washington meeting with somebody about funding, I think, and we met in the afternoon on the mall. I don't know what we were talking about, in fact I don't remember anything else about the visit, but you said one thing that stuck in my mind. Now I remember it vividly, after finding this coffee.

You said something like, "If you can't see that the entire universe is probably organized and fully inhabited by beings far more intelligent than we are, then you still believe the world is flat, right? You're repeating the same mistake made by everyone in the general public during the time of Copernicus. They were completely wrong about how celestial bodies worked, and when Copernicus showed them the truth they didn't believe it. That's us today," you said.

Blake: That's right. Today we're repeating this Copernican error in the spiritual arena. We think Earth people are the only spiritual beings there are. We know a good deal of truth about celestial bodies in the physical arena, but we still think the universe is empty in the spiritual arena. And, of course, the Copernican Error makes us self-centered and ethnocentric in virtually every arena from the deeply personal to the local, the regional, the social, the cultural, the religious, the national, and the planetary.

Evan: At the time I thought you were a little batty. I wondered where you got such a preposterous idea, but I didn't dwell on it. We just went on talking about other things and I forgot about it. It wasn't until years later when I first drank this coffee that the idea came crashing back into my head and this time I saw what you meant. It made sense to me that there would be a civilization filled with beings out there living in the physical universe.

Blake: What was going on? I'd like to hear about it.

Evan started his story easily but seriously.

Evan: Okay. Well, it's a pretty interesting story. A guy I've known for a long time called me and wanted me to consider helping him market a new strain of coffee he developed. He's an expert at growing and blending coffee. He and I worked together at Paschal Foods back in the '80s and '90s.

When I went to see him he was in Paraguay. He had been working with some growers to develop new coffee strains that might lead to something they can use to compete in the export markets. They had come up with something and they wanted me to help them market it.

It was a nice trip. He paid part of my expenses and Jennifer went with me. It was a relaxed, laid-back vacation. But the second day I was there he asked me to meet him at his apartment in the city. He was rather secretive about it. When I got there it was only the two of us. He wanted me to sample this coffee he had stumbled upon and had told no one else about. We drank a cup of the coffee and ate some scones. I said I liked how the coffee tasted but I wasn't sure it was very different from most other coffee.

Then he got up, took a plastic dropper from the counter, and said, "Let's have another cup and this time we'll put a couple of drops." He was moving around the counter between the kitchen and the sitting/eating area getting the coffee pot. He was happy and animated. There was a kind of excited gleam in his eye.

"See if you can tell any difference between this and other coffees when it has this in it."

We drank the coffee with the mysterious drops and ate another scone. Nothing was different and I told myself of course I should not expect there to be some difference immediately. I waited and changed the subject. I was just about ready to decide it was all a bust when I remembered what you said.

I have no idea why that memory came bursting into my mind. At first I thought it was completely unrelated to the coffee. But for some reason I found myself quite interested in the idea that the universe was fully populated and organized and operated in a meaningful, orderly way.

All of a sudden I couldn't get the idea out of my mind. I was fascinated and quite excited. I remembered that I got the idea from you and I wondered how you had come up with it.

As I thought, more meanings and questions related to the idea kept pouring into my mind. I wondered how much more you knew about it. I asked myself why it wasn't known by everyone. Probably we're just now coming into readiness to know about it. We know about UFOs and aliens but we don't believe in them. Aren't we slowly becoming more accepting of them, though, just as we're becoming more accepting of the idea that there are other inhabited planets like ours? Probably that's how it will be with this.

I thought maybe there were a lot of people who thought this way these days, even though it makes sense that the public hasn't heard about it yet. Usually, at the beginning of something like this it gets rejected and laughed at. I thought maybe that's where we are today. As you said, we would normally reject something like this in the same way Copernicus was rejected.

I started talking about the idea with my friend there and he asked me where I got such an idea. He said that if it is true it's a big game changer. It was the first time he had ever entertained such a notion. I told him about you and he said he'd like to meet you. He got very excited by the idea, as I had. He started talking very loud and fast.

    Then he started telling me that this was an example of the kind of thing that happens with people when they drink the coffee with the drops in it. I was struck by this statement. It really hit me that maybe this very wild realization is facilitated by the coffee. I began to wonder if the idea was really as true as it seemed.

    Until then I had assumed it *is*. It was a bit sobering to think it's not really true but "just the coffee." To this day, however, I still believe it's true deep in my heart. But I really need to talk with you about it. Do you believe it's true?

Blake: Absolutely. I'm sure of it.

Evan: Why?

Blake sits silent . . . thinking for an uncomfortable few seconds. Then he carefully begins to speak.
Because I have very good evidence that it's true.

Evan: Of course. What is your evidence?

    Again Blake was awkwardly silent. Evan looked at him expectantly. As the silence continued, Evan became uncomfortable so he began to fill the silence with questions.

Evan: Why is it so hard to tell me? Is it some kind of secret? Is it not really good evidence? Come on man, tell me.

Blake: Look, I want to go very slow right here. You are excited right now but the conversation has come to a point where we need to go slow and consider very carefully.

Evan: Why all the intrigue? Is there good evidence or not?
Evan is thinking that Blake can give him some new scientific studies that have recently been released or something. But Blake is right—Evan is very excited and he's not particularly known for his patience anyway.

Blake: At first you may not consider it good evidence but, I need you to go slow and suspend judgment until you hear the whole story and really give this a good look. It's important to thoroughly consider everything.

 Blake began to talk about his clients and that the very thing they needed was the thing they didn't consider and that people did this all the time.
 Evan knew that Blake is a psychotherapist and a very good one. He understood, at least a little bit, that Blake helps people change and reshape their lives. They've talked about these things a lot over the years, but Evan had never taken Blake's techniques and theories very seriously or, at least, not very personally. He thought he understood Blake's work very well and he had used a lot of his ideas mildly in his own life, but he really didn't understand as well as he thought he did.

Evan: So now you're treating me like one of your clients, huh? Is this what you say to them when you're trying to tell one of them something that you know will sound preposterous but you think they need to consider it anyway?

Blake: Well, yes.

Evan: Well, what if it really is preposterous and you're just leading them down the primrose path to hell in a handbasket?

Blake: Is that what you think? Do you think the whole idea of an organized, populated, governed universe is really preposterous and I'm just trying to take you to hell in a handbasket?

Evan: Well, no, but you're being so reluctant and mysterious about the evidence and, besides, my not thinking it's preposterous could be just the coffee.

Blake: Ah, is that what this stuff is you put in the coffee? It's stuff that makes preposterous things seem sensible, right?

Evan: Well, uh, no, but maybe. To me the coffee does the opposite. It makes true things truer, or it makes you more confident in true things. What it actually does, though, is the big question. That's the reason I asked you to come here. I need you to help me find out whether or not this coffee helps people realize.

    At times it seems like that's what it does—it makes preposterous things seem right. And other times it seems like something that just makes you see the *real true* heart of the matter. It seems to *enhance* your ability to see the truth. It seems to give you clear *realizations*.

Blake: Well, you know, that's pretty wild coffee if it does that, especially if it does it all the time. One of the main things I try to help people understand, especially my clients, is that psychotherapy is about learning to improve the quality of the truth you perceive and the truth by which you're living. And that's what it seems like realization does—it improves the quality of your perception of the truth.

Understanding one's self and one's psychology well enough to improve requires waking up to see what's *really* going on—see what you're truly believing and expecting and how it's messing you up. This state of being awake seeing your errors can also help you see something *new* or something *more* about what's important. It involves having a realization. A realization usually involves seeing something more or something new about something you already know.

Realization is the quintessential wake-up experience. A realization expands your spirit. Every time you feel yourself having a realization, you are feeling your spirit grow and develop. When you have a realization, you know you had it even though you may play it down or ignore it. You know you had it because you feel it. It increases your enthusiasm and makes you at least a little bit fascinated about this thing you're realizing right now. Waking up means improving the quality and the accuracy of the truth that is before you and it's basically *the same thing* as realization.

Entire populations of people and races also have wake-up experiences, and they make great leaps forward in their understanding of reality in a relatively short time. This is what happened in the time of Copernicus when, in a relatively short period of time, it became public knowledge and was accepted by everyone that the Sun does not move across the sky each day but rather the Earth turns and makes it *look as though* the Sun is moving. After that we rapidly figured out how the mechanisms of the solar system worked and literally everyone came to understand it.

Maybe that's what the coffee does—it makes those who drink it have a realization or at least it potentiates your ability to have one.

Expanding one's thought and understanding in any framework is a big major part of life. I try to help people see that they're wrong most of the time. They may be *right,* but they're also wrong and being wrong is good because then they can make correction and achieve helpful change. Seeing one's error is priceless in helping one learn, grow, and expand.

Believe me, Evan, if you have discovered a coffee that really does help people have realizations, then you have discovered a tremendously valuable and powerful tool.

For a little bit of time that could have been any length of time at all, the two friends sat and looked at each other, each one thinking his own thoughts about it and reflecting over the entire situation.

Evan: Well, I think that might very well be what we have here. The coffee with the drops in it facilitates realization. How do we find out for sure?

Blake: You mean, how do we measure the effect of the coffee? It's really the effect of the clear liquid drops you put in the coffee. What is that stuff anyway? Is it okay with the Food and Drug Administration?

Evan: We're waiting on formal approval from the FDA on that. But we know it's going to be okay because those ingredients are already being used in some popular energy drinks. My partner knew about them already and just *by chance* discovered the effect when mixed with the coffee. They are two very simple and popular ingredients. He just put them together with a binding agent. And they do seem to have more of an effect when you put them in *this* coffee rather than other coffees.

Blake: You mean the actual strain of coffee makes a difference?

Evan: Yes, it does seem to. This is another thing we would like to test, though. And that's going to be your job, isn't it?

Blake looked at him intensely and silently. All of a sudden he *realized* what Evan was asking him to do. He was becoming quite excited, and his excitement had a large modicum of eustress mixed in. He felt activated and anxious in an excited kind of way. He was scared but also very happy to find himself involved in this "new coffee" business.

Blake's interest in this project was exploding inside him. He was beginning to wake up to a huge number of implications racing through his mind. He could see that this was potentially a very big and powerful project. It was both exciting and scary. He saw it was the kind of thing that can lead in a hundred different directions. It could be a positive substance that actually helps people grow. It also could expand the general public's understanding of the nature of the universe. There are a huge number of related things here.

There was the potential for defining realization and exploring in great detail the inner psychological process of wake-up. There was also great potential in realizing how many people resonate positively to the idea of an organized and populated universe civilization as Evan knew existed. It was also quite noticeable that the concept was much more favorable to Evan. This project could help the idea become more familiar and favorable to many others.

This coffee could become a huge tool for teaching people about the process of realization and self-discovery (i.e., spiritual development or psychotherapy). It could also help a vast number of people get a convincing glimpse of the *real* universe kingdom. If they could get enough of a glimpse to see that it's *real* they will be shocked by how similar it is to the system we have right now right here on Earth, while at the same time it's so *very* different. It's different in that its rulers are truly positive and enlightened so they can be trusted to do what's truly best for everyone. What a shocking circumstance *that* is.

If a great majority of Earth's population were hit by the reality of the universe civilization the way Evan was when he first drank the coffee, what a huge difference it would make.

Blake (in his private, inner self): Wow! What an amazing thing this is. It really is much, much more far-reaching than I ever suspected. It's *an incredible opportunity*. It's a chance to teach and study realization. It's also a chance to show people The Urantia Book and have them *realize* with much greater clarity what it is and *that* there is an actual universe civilization here in space that is way beyond anything our people know about. It's an opportunity to help the world *realize* that the Kingdom of Heaven is *real*.

The Kingdom of Heaven is *real* and the only thing needed to make it become formally acknowledged and established on Earth is for the people of Earth to realize the truth about it.

Blake's cell phone began to vibrate and sing its song in his pocket. He brought it out and answered. It was his wife, Lacy.

Blake: Hello, girl.

Lacy: Hey, mister. Did you make it up there today?

Blake: Yeah, I'm here. Evan and Jennifer are still breathing. I haven't seen Jennifer yet. I guess I'll see her later tonight.

Lacy: Well, tell her hi for me when you see her. Tell Evan, too. Have you decided when you're coming home yet?

Blake: No, I haven't decided that yet but I don't think it'll be tomorrow. Evan really does have something going on here that's pretty interesting. In fact it's *very* interesting. I'm pretty surprised. I can't describe it to you right now; I'll tell you more when I get home. I guess I'll be coming home either Friday or Saturday. Right now, I guess, I'm thinking more like Saturday.

Lacy: Yeah, well, I can't wait to hear what's so interesting. I guess I'll see you when you get here.

Blake: I'll call you again tomorrow as things develop. Don't be antsy. Are the boys okay?

Lacy: Oh yeah. Everybody's fine here. Just let us know.

Blake: I will. Have a good night tonight.

Chapter Three

The Group

For a little while Blake is deep in his thoughts. Evan had gotten up and gone behind the counter to pay attention to some business. Blake unzips a pocket of his backpack, reaches in and pulls out a small note pad and a pen. He makes some notes about what to have on a questionnaire. The questions are constructed in a way that evaluates how much those who drink the coffee with the drops are realizing. The noise level from people talking and moving around the coffee shop is lively. People are laughing and chattering buoyantly among themselves.

There's the occasional voice talking louder than the others perhaps to someone across the room or loud because of some excitement or being loud is just how their nature.

Voice: Did you talk to Mario last night?

And the answer is spoken by someone quieter, so Blake can't hear.

A voice from the group: Hey, Grolley, who won the game last night?

Grolley (answering from across the room): They did!

Blake begins to pay attention to the customers and workers in the place. That's how he is—he enjoys watching groups of people interact in places like this. He can tell a lot about them from watching them closely. He feels warm and close to these people. A budding affection for them has emerged inside of him. Maybe it's because he knows they are drinking the coffee. It's hard to say exactly why, but he appreciates that they seem to be accepting him.

Toward the front and over to the side of the room, a motley group of erstwhile lounge chairs are arranged in a circle around a large table that is approximately coffee table height. There are ten chairs and an equally motley group of maybe twelve or thirteen people of both sexes variously sitting, standing, and moving around this area. Blake had noticed them earlier. Now he watches them with focused attention spinning trial theories in his mind about who they are and what their business is.

Blake (in his private, inner self): What a bunch this is—regular people on New York's Lower East Side. Regular people in a world-famous neighborhood. This place is pretty popular. Good for Evan and Jennifer. It seems like many of these are regulars who spend a lot of time here and probably have friendships among them that go back many years. They're obviously familiar with each other and pretty smart, vivacious, and witty.

Someone says: I don't think I'm going to have any extra drops tonight.

Someone else says: This coffee has been wearing out my brain.

Female voice: Oh, come on, you need a lot of the coffee. How are you going to catch up?

One person stands out particularly in the group. He's a lean Latino man with wild, dark curly hair. His voice is not exactly loud but strong and clear so it's easy to hear a lot of what he says. He seems to be a major leader of the group, a sociometric star.

Most people in the group approach him often and keep him in the center of the conversation. He cooperates with this by being very animated and talking to everyone. Blake even knows his name because it has been used so much by various other members of the group. His name is Renaldo.

People sort of lightly swirl around Renaldo. They wouldn't want anyone to know it, but they seem to get a kind of satisfaction or gratification from being around him, getting his attention every now and then, and knowing they have access to him. Renaldo pays attention to each of them when it is precisely appropriate.

"I know, I wonder about that," he might say, or "You guys are always playing around" or "C'mon now, don't do me that way." He answers their questions, gives them praise or advice, joins in, laughs with them, and gives personal attention to things they consider important.

This little group of regulars gives the coffee shop an added level of legitimacy and solidity. They are really humming right now. They are carrying on their business of being the main group of regulars. They tell jokes, give out information, and keep up an apparently entertaining conversation. They are maintaining a lively repartee when Evan comes out from behind the counter and stops by their group. He says a few words to some of them. They all immediately stop and look over in Blake's direction.

Blake (in his private, inner self): Uh, oh. What's this? He told them about me. It looks like he's told them about me before.

Someone says: Blake?

Another voice: He's here? Really?

Their words tumble out.
Evan is now looking and pointing over in Blake's direction. Everyone in the group is looking. Evan begins to beckon for Blake to come over. He's scooping his hand and forearm from Blake's direction to theirs like a cop directing traffic. Blake gets up and begins to move over to their front corner of the shop.
A sort of loud, fast, chaotic round of introductions begins. People say their names and greet him, "Hello." "Hey, how are you?" "We've heard a lot about you," "Glad to meet you," and so on.
Blake goes around and shakes people's hands and says, "Glad to meet you."

A guy named Winfry gives a little explanation about what Evan said about him when he told his story about first finding the coffee.

Dede: Do you really believe the universe is organized and governed by highly advanced beings and populated by trillions of intelligent beings at least as intelligent as we are?

Dede is a dark-haired woman who looks Italian. Blake couldn't tell if she was challenging him or not. He nodded his head.

Dede: Where did you get this idea?

Blake: From my studies. I've been studying this for a long time.

It's an answer he often gives when talking with people who aren't really interested or when it's a situation not conducive to a more in-depth look. It worked now. Blake isn't really ready to jump into a big conversation right now and this answer allows others in the group to say things and bring up comments or other questions that were easier.
Shortly Blake came back to Dede looking intently at her.

Blake: Dede, do you doubt the idea?

Dede: Well I don't know. I would like it to be true. If it were and everyone knew it, everything would be very different. But, it's probably just wishful thinking. From one perspective it does seem reasonable, but it certainly isn't commonly believed.

Paco: Most people would say you're a kook if they knew you thought that.

Maggie (tossing in): So, who cares if they think you're a kook. People think you're a kook for just living on the Lower East Side.

Renaldo: This is a big thing, though. If it's true, it's a very big thing. If people begin to see that it's true—the universe, organized, populated, and governed—that'll make a huge difference in who we are and how we live our lives. It's as big as when people began to see that the world was round instead of flat back in the time of Copernicus.

   Everybody was quiet for a few moments. They were thinking about what Renaldo said--thoughtfully digesting it. Some of them were having realizations about the enormity as Renaldo pointed it out. Some of them had been drinking the coffee.
   Blake was surprised and impressed with what Renaldo said. He could see why Renaldo was the sociometric leader. Everyone respected him.

Blake: That's right. Suppose everyone knew that Earth is just one of thousands of other planets that have races of people very similar to us who are in various stages of development. Suppose they have unique histories—

different specific paths their people take to achieve their development and reach the place where they know about the universe system and their place in it.

Suppose these facts were acknowledged in the public media and our television journalists talked about it as though it's an accepted thing or at least accepted by many. Suppose there's an open broadcast channel between our planet and the system capital and every day or at least quite often there are television stories about things happening on other planets in our system—and other systems beyond ours.

Carlene: Wow. This really is a big idea, isn't it? You've thought a lot about this. You think they have television communication between planets? It sounds like a science fiction story. Do you think that's the kind of civilization it is? Do they have advertising?

Blake (intrigued by her question): I think it's a civilization that is very like ours in some ways and very different from ours in other ways. Maybe the biggest and most important difference is that in the culture of the universe system, service flows downward. In our culture, service flows upward.

Carlene (her curiosity really piqued by this idea): What do you mean?

Blake: In the universe the higher beings serve the lower beings. Those who are stronger and wiser and have more resources serve those less blessed. But here we believe the lower should serve the higher. Here on Earth the weaker, the less intelligent, and the ones with fewer resources serve the ones who are stronger, smarter and have more resources. We believe this is correct. To us it seems sensible that it should be this way. But that's not how they see it in the universe kingdom.

Theirs is a much more advanced civilization than ours. Their values are very different. Their civilization is very old and their leaders are far beyond ours intellectually and in spiritual development.

In the universe system they are much more aware that they are living in an eternal system. I don't know if they have advertising but that's a great question. If they do have advertising, I'm sure it's very different from ours—there's no exaggeration and lying like there Is here. I'm pretty sure their communication system does not have to be paid for by advertising.

Liz: This is amazing. The more you talk, the harder it is for me to think it's really true. Or if it is true, it's deeply upsetting somehow.

Gary (sitting right next to Liz): It's utterly ridiculous. If this civilization in the sky is actually real, why do we know nothing about it? And why does it sound so preposterous just on the face of it?

Blake: How much do you think is in the universe that's very important and we know nothing about it? We tend to think there's not much we don't know, but that's because we're so asleep. The opposite is actually true. Isn't it arrogant to think we should know about everything?

Or maybe we're just naive. Maybe we don't understand The "Prime Directive"—that we are a planet or a group of races in training. It's against the rules for celestials to reveal things to us that we should discover for ourselves such as the truth about them. We'll know about them when we realize the truth about them.

Gary: But we have to ask ourselves, what are the chances, you know? What are the chances that this guy Blake is really onto something incredibly momentous? Or is he just crazy? Or has he just fallen for a hoax? Is he even maybe scamming us in some way? Aren't the probabilities on the side of the hoax?

Blake: Not if you know what I know. Not if you've studied what I've studied. That is a good question though—is it a hoax? And we should do a good, honest job of answering this question.

Liz: Well, I don't think Blake is scamming us. But it is some wild stuff I'm hearing. Don't be bothered by Gary (she gives Blake a knowing look). He's a skeptic. He's pessimistic about most everything. That's just the way he is.

Blake: I understand. I know these things are hard to swallow when you first hear them. But the more detail we explore, the bigger the realization gets, and the bigger the veracity of the reality gets. It's natural for our minds to explore and it's natural to be skeptical. But it's also very appropriate to either prove the skepticism correct or reduce it by doing our homework.

If what I'm saying is true? People will naturally want to know about these other planets and what's happening with them—what they've been through and what they've learned. Have they had wars and cataclysms? Have they had an industrial revolution? What do they think about God? Likewise, we will want to know a little history about them and we'll wonder what they are saying about us. Can you imagine what a different context that would be for our concept of the universe?

Isabelle: Now that you put it that way, it makes me think it must not be true because I can't imagine living in that kind of world. It seems that literally everybody will be half off their rocker.

Lester (who had been sitting there quietly but intently listening to the conversation): Of course, there are a lot of people who will not accept this. They would say it's sheer craziness to think that the universe is inhabited and organized in a governed society.

Raul: They would say just what Isabelle said—they wouldn't be able to imagine such a thing.

Josie: Isabelle is saying she doesn't want it to be true. It would change our concept of the world so much that we couldn't stand it. It's just too radical a departure from the way we're used to seeing things.

Monet: Yeah, that's what I think.

Audrey: Me too.

Carlene: Aw, come on. Just let your imagination go a little. Don't you think we'd adjust to the whole thing once we got used to it? Look at what a great thing it is if it's true. We just can't believe it could be true. If it is, it's a vast improvement of what we've got. It's a real heaven. We say all the time that we want things to be good and right and perfect, but we don't really want that do we? We don't really think it's possible.

Blake: Something that's very important is the assumptions we hold in the back of our mind—the deep, unconscious mind. These assumptions make up our personal inner context. We're rarely aware of them, but they determine everything else we think and believe. People in our culture believe space is cold, dark, and empty except for some physical elements like stars, asteroids, meteors, planets, and moons. So we rule out things like beings and organized governments automatically.

When you consider it, that doesn't make any sense. We may not be able to see or have evidence of the beings and governments, but we should be scientifically savvy enough to know we can't rule them out, especially in a universe like this one that is so extremely and amazingly ordered and intelligent.

Carlene: I don't think we can stand the idea of an actual heaven on Earth. We talk about "easy street" and a "golden age" or dream of Shangri La and so on, but we don't truly want anything like that. We love our big mess we've got here. We don't want to give it up. We don't want what Blake is talking about to be true.

Blake: We have a saying in my field: "People choose known hells and reject unknown heavens." Isn't that what's happening here? There's an intuitive sense that a global realization about this very astonishing notion that space is populated and governed would require huge, scary changes in us and our way of life. We just can't go there.

Gary: A lot of people are surely going to reject the idea of a populated, governed universe. And I guess that could be because it's such a radical departure from what we believe now. It's so unknown—inconceivable! Maybe that is the basic reason.

Blake: A huge crowd of people is going to reject this idea and not just reject it, but reject it *vehemently*. They can only accept the kind of heaven they've been taught about—the phony and unrealistic kind. They don't care if regular ideas of heaven don't fit with what they know about reality. They cling to the old ideas that are phony. The old ideas are accepted because they're what have been accepted and taken for granted as they are for a long time. They reject a modern, realistic idea of heaven because that concept is venturing into the unknown. They think it challenges the past and makes them lose something precious.

The common concepts of heaven are either about "pie in the sky by and by" or some alien civilization we're scared of being destroyed by. People are scared of losing everything they don't want to give up. They don't see a positive gain in any of the things they've been taught, but that's okay. At least the commonly accepted construct is familiar. Yet the truth is that the true heaven is very positive and an incredible improvement of what there is now. Plus, it's completely realistic. That's the idea that scares people most.

Liz: That's right, you're a therapist, aren't you? Evan told us you are a psychologist and he wants you to study people's reaction to the coffee. He wants to learn more about its effect. What do you think is going on with the coffee?

Blake: I'm not sure but it seems to help with something that I think is very important. That's the psychological phenomenon of realization. To experience the phenomenon of waking up and seeing what's actually going on is very important psychologically. It is major realization. It's particularly important to wake up inside in your personal inner world. This is the key psychological process to making improvement and becoming better. It's the key to psychotherapy. Realization means waking up.

Carlene: And you think the coffee makes people have this experience of waking up or realizing? What if it's not an experience of insight or seeing the truth? What if it's an experience of putting on rose-colored glasses and seeing things more positively but not necessarily truthfully?

Blake: Well, I don't know. That certainly is important. We'll have to figure out a way to test and see if it is enhancing people's experience of truth or if it is something else? What do all of you think? Do you believe the coffee helps you have true realizations, or is it just a counterfeit truth people are experiencing?

There was a little period of silence here. The majority of the people in the group had experienced something positive after drinking the coffee with the drops, but none of them had thought about it in such precise detail. Whether or not the coffee actually brings about a realization or a clear and enhanced view of truth was a much more exact question than they had entertained before. They were caught off guard and felt off balance.

Finally Winfry spoke up.

Winfry: Well, I hadn't thought about it in quite those terms, but I guess the notion that the coffee facilitates realization is a possibility with me. It does usually stir up a positive experience for me and when I think back over it, my experience is that I usually get into thinking about something that struck me as very interesting. I start having a dialog with myself about aspects of things that are fascinating and impressive. I'm realizing right now about realization. I can see it is very important.

Carlene: Yeah, that's somewhat true for me, too. That is a realization, isn't it?

Winfry: And it's not like smoking a joint or taking some drugs. I stay very normal in my general awareness, like drinking regular Folgers, you might say, but with the new coffee I focus in on something that grabs my attention and I become very impressed by some aspect of it.

Lester: Yeah, waking up is a good way to describe it. I feel very much like I'm in my same situation without any of my faculties being altered, but my awareness has just been sharpened. Most of the time my interest in something is stirred up and I see new aspects of it.

Renaldo: Yeah, I can very much see how you would say that the coffee facilitates realization.

Gary: Not me. Nothing happens to me when I drink the coffee. My experience is that it's not different from water or milk or a Coke or some other coffee.

Raul: That's what happens for me.

Liz: I feel good and, like, everything's cool when I drink the coffee but I don't know that I can say I'm having realizations.

(Liz is a woman who seems very sane and normal.)

Liz: I will say that it seems a little more stimulating than other coffees. I'm going to start paying attention now to see if I'm having more realizations.

A guy named Michael was sitting over by the wall. He is a pleasant looking guy with curly, graying hair. After listening for a long time he spoke up.

Michael: I've been thinking about it since we've been talking and I think the coffee has indeed functioned as a realization facilitator for me. Since Blake got here today I started thinking about this idea of a populated, organized, and governed universe and that it was really far-fetched and not very likely, but now I'm much more willing to say that maybe it is possible.
Maybe it does make sense that the universe would be like that. It makes a lot more sense about God and notions regarding eternity and the afterlife, and the traditional ideas held by various religions. When I look at that, I see it has been a process of realization and the only thing that's changed for me since I've been here today is drinking the coffee.
Also, when I think back on the last couple of months since I first started coming here, I can remember that I've

been having a lot of insights. For instance, one thing I've just been realizing today is about the old saying, "Life is Hard." I've been realizing that life always feels difficult to some extent, even when I'm not having any challenges to meet. I mean that in actuality, life is not hard. I pretty much get up every morning and go through the day and I know how to do it and it's not hard. Yet, if I look at it a certain way, it has a component of difficulty.

There are always things you have to make yourself do and that feels hard, especially in the beginning when you're starting it. I think that's pretty true for everybody—rich and poor, smart and dumb, talented and untalented. You have to make yourself do certain necessary things you'd rather not do and that always feels hard.

Carlene (a tall, thin, attractive lady): You know, a lot of people believe the concept of a populated and governed universe already. I was talking to a guy in my office today and I mentioned the idea of the universe being totally ordered and organized and governed and he said he completely believed that.

But then when I started going into detail such as people working and having projects to do and the various planets communicating among themselves and having transportation technologies, then it started becoming more real and he became skeptical and less sure it's true. I thought this was rather peculiar. He believed a less real picture but doubted a more real picture. That's a familiar psychological construct, isn't it? I've been thinking about this all day; maybe I'm having a realization.

Grolley: And, you know, I've been having a realization about all the things we take so seriously all the time. A huge number of the things that we take very seriously are somewhat silly and unimportant. Take, for instance, what other people think about us or where we're going on vacation or why we keep making the same mistakes.

A couple of weeks ago my wife and I were going out on Friday night with friends to get baseball tickets from another friend. But then after we made our plans we couldn't get the tickets and I got so upset. I got all uptight and worried about what I was going to do about providing our entertainment.

Of course everything worked out fine and we went to a play in the Village. Then I started having this realization about how I had made the thing so very important. I'm having more realizations like that tonight. So much of what I do in my life is so unimportant but I make it extremely important. I wonder what the coffee does do.

Renaldo: Yeah, that's a really good question. What are some of your ideas, Blake? How do you go about designing a study to determine what's happening with the coffee?

Blake: Well, one idea is to ask everybody who drinks the coffee about some proposition like what we've been discussing—that the universe is populated, organized, and governed. We can ask both those drinking it with the drops and those drinking it without the drops and see how much the two groups differ in the degree to which they see that the possibility could be true.

Renaldo: Will that work all right? You don't really know if it is true.

Blake: Personally, I am convinced that it's true (he was looking intently at Renaldo), but I'm not sure if we're talking here about realizing it's true or just realizing it's a possibility. Given most people's various frameworks and their situations, just realizing it's a possibility may be the best they can do.

Gary (being the skeptic): So let me see if I understand this. You're saying that the world needs to realize that the universe is populated, organized, and governed and with the help of the coffee, we here on the Lower East Side could help this realization spread, right? What a grandiose scheme.

Liz: Whoa, hey now, hang on. Let's not blow this into something a lot bigger than it is. We're not saying Blake's trying to manipulate the world. Let's just look at what we have right here in front of us. This realization idea is intensely interesting to me and, as I understand it, we're just talking about realizing that the populated, governed universe concept is possible. Blake, you say realization is the key. How is realization the key?

Blake: All psychological problems are the result of error. Thus, solving the problem or making improvement regarding the problem comes from correcting error.

Except for medical problems, all human problems are psychological problems and all psychological problems are due to errors of thinking and judgment, especially errors of assumption that people make in their deep, unconscious mind. The unconscious mind or the "deep mind" is where our values, beliefs, and assumptions are centered. They are responsible for the way we see the world. They form our context and shape our thoughts and actions. They are filled with error.

Usually the errors involve selfish egocentric desire. That's why I call the basic, most fundamental error the Copernican Error. Each of us do in our personal life the same thing our entire population was doing as a group in Copernicus' time when it was believed that the people of Earth were the center of the universe and the Sun circled the Earth rather than the Earth circling the Sun.

Lester: Ah, the old ego. Being hugely in the clutches of our ego, that's what Eckhart Tolle talks about. I guess I've had a realization about ego and how very difficult it is to see how much our ego distorts our perception.

Blake: Right. The ego makes us think things are false when they're not. Or it tells us things are true when they are not. Or it makes us slant our interpretations of our experience in ways that favor our interests. These are highly personalized directions that are distortions of what's actually there. The ego is the root of why such a vast majority of our assumptions are erroneous.

When we're in the parking lot at the store looking for a parking spot and one opens up right in front of the store door, near where we are, we think that's something God did for us because we're so special. Or when some guy who wants to drive faster than we do comes roaring around us and cuts in front of us very close we get very mad at him and project that he's mad at us. This is because we over-personalize things.

Liz: You mean God *didn't* provide that parking space? People who think like that make me chuckle.

Robert: You're the one making people chuckle.

At this point Evan comes out from the kitchen and stands by the door listening to the conversation. He says nothing but is very interested in what he's hearing.

Blake: We all know that getting life right involves the repudiation, management, and transformation of egocentric desire. These errors of ego—you could call it our selfish prejudices—create problems when we aren't aware that we're indulging in those desires and we're operating erroneously.

We are not aware of either the egocentric desire or the error of assumption. In order to make improvement, we must wake up and see our egocentric desire and/or our mistaken assumption and correct it. This is done through realization.

We may believe we're right or justified in being negative or hating someone because of something he or she said or did when we are actually just jealous and want to best them. Or we may believe we are right or justified in hating a person on the basis of race or ethnic background or the person's home state or religion. In reality we're in competition with them.

We may believe we are correct and justified by objective facts when we condemn people for the way they dress or how they look or how they talk or how fat they are, but what if we're not right? What are we going to do? We're not going to get better or grow or make progress until we realize and admit our error to ourselves and make a correction.

We may feel we are right in making the assumption that there is no way the universe could be populated, organized, and governed. We may believe we are right in making the assumption that there is no book or other evidence sent here from that government that would be a revelation ordained by them.

But if the universe civilization, as we are talking about it, is really there—if it's really true—then we're going to be wrong about reality in a big way until we realize we're wrong and make correction.

Carlene: Oh. Is that what you're saying, Blake? Are you saying that the universe civilization exists and official evidence has been sent to us from them to demonstrate the authenticity of their existence?

Blake (after thinking for a few seconds): Yes, that is what I'm saying. That is, in fact, what has happened. Convincing evidence has been sent from the highest levels of the official universe government to reveal their existence to us.

So, Gary, you're mistaken when you say we know nothing about this civilization. Some of us do know about it because we've seen the evidence. There are probably around a half million of us who have seen this evidence. That's not really a very large percentage of the population of Earth but it is a fairly large absolute number of people.

Monet: Can you show us this evidence?

Lester: Yeah, I'd really like to see that evidence.

Liz: Me too.

Carlene: Of course, we all would.

Blake: How about if I do that tomorrow night? I'm a little beat tonight and I'd like to take the load off and get a little rest. I've had a long day.

Evan (from the kitchen door): Do you want to leave now? Renaldo says he'll show you how to get to my apartment. I have to stay here a while longer to get some things done. Jennifer and Claire are there and I'll come along as soon as I'm clear here. How's that?

Blake (looking over at Renaldo): That'll be fine.

(I'll be glad to meet Renaldo. I can get to know him some while we're walking.)

The people in the group began to mill around and say friendly good-byes to Blake. He responded warmly to them as well. There were several mini-conversations between him and various individuals. He went over and asked Evan about a couple of details having to do with negotiating the evening at his house.

He was preparing to start out on the walk to Evan's house with Renaldo when Lester spoke up in a voice more audible than the many other smaller conversations.

Lester (enthusiastically): So, I can't wait! We'll all meet here again tomorrow night to hear what Blake has to say about evidence.

Raul: Hear, hear!

Raul, though pessimistic, was getting very interested.

Liz: Yes, I very much want to hear about it, too.

Audrey: Oh, shoot. I can't come tomorrow. I'll call you, Katherine. Will you be here tomorrow?

Katherine: Yes, I think so. If not, we can call Alicia or Dede.

The women were all looking at each other and nodding to confirm that someone would be available who could later be called if there was a need. Everyone was milling around talking with each other again.

Blake and Renaldo both began moving toward the door.

Renaldo (connecting with Blake somewhere in the middle of the room): It's a good night for a brisk little walk.

Blake: How far is it?

Renaldo: Not far, maybe ten minutes. I like this breeze.

They had come out of the shop and were walking down Bowery Street toward Houston Street. Evan lived several blocks down Houston.

Renaldo: Wow, that was some interesting stuff in there tonight. It's funny how many different views there are on this thing about the universe.

Blake: I'd really like to hear your view, not just on the universe though. I'd like to hear your version of the entire conversation tonight. What do you think was being said there?

Renaldo (after thinking for a few moments): Well, I think there were basically two things being talked about: The first thing was the idea of the universe being populated, organized, and governed. The second thing is the thing of realization. Both topics actually go together because the main issue about the first topic—the universe being populated and governed—is how much has been realized about it being true. The opinion of each person there varied widely about this.

This second topic of realization is essentially about how much. It's not just whether one believes the new theory of the universe, it's how much does one believe it. How much one believes it depends on how much you realize that it is or could be true. That's one of the things being said about realizations—they are a matter of quantity.

How much do you realize something? You can realize something in different amounts. In this case it's how much do you believe or realize that the universe is populated, organized, and governed.

Blake: Yes. That's really a good, succinct statement about our discussion. Right now it is a major thing on the agenda for our entire planet Earth to wake up and realize the true structure of the universe we live in. It is totally populated, completely organized, and wisely, positively governed.

The two men continued to talk as they moved toward Evan's house on Houston Street. It was a cool, balmy night in September and there was plenty of activity on the street—many sights, smells, and sounds. People were walking at different paces, in all directions, many who were not walking at all made the sidewalk a place to be on its own, the home of the homeless, not just a way to go somewhere.

Either alone or talking to each other, some folks were sitting on the pavement leaning back against something like a building or a pole or a stoop. Quite a few others lay on benches that would be their beds for the night. They had to stake out their claim early if they wanted to hold the bench.

Blake and Renaldo were absorbed in the things they were still talking about left over from the coffee shop discussion, but they couldn't entirely ignore the business being conducted by the characters on the street. There were so many of them so different from one another.

There were a thousand fascinating stories there within just a few blocks. But to Blake and Renaldo, few were more interesting than the one they were discussing and none implied an impact on such a scale and scope as to involve the entire Earth waking up to its place in the universe in as important a manner as the wake-up ushered in by Copernicus six hundred years ago.

Renaldo stopped all of a sudden and looked intensely at Blake.

Renaldo: I know about your evidence. It's The Urantia Book, isn't it?

Blake: Yes, you know about it, huh?

Renaldo: Yes, I know about it. But I haven't read it. I actually haven't paid much attention to it. I just have a friend who showed it to me a little while ago and told me some very basic things about it. You could say I haven't realized what it is until today. That happened in the coffee shop tonight while I was listening to the conversation and, I suppose, drinking the coffee. I put it all together and woke up to it tonight.

Blake: Before that, you were asleep to it. I don't know which is more interesting: people when they're asleep to something important or when they wake up. Both phenomena are fascinating as hell.

Both men looked at each other silently for a moment and then Renaldo reached out to shake hands with Blake.

Renaldo: This whole business is incredibly exciting to me!

They each grabbed the other's upper right arm with their left hands and smiled very big.

Renaldo (light dancing in his eyes): I'm so pleased to meet you, sir.

Blake was a bit shaken.

Blake: I have the same great gratitude about meeting you, Renaldo.

After a moment of intensity they started walking again.

Renaldo: I guess we'd better get on over to Evan's place.

There was a sea of vehicles, and at least a blue million of cab customers stepping out into the street waving and whistling trying to make a connection. Every couple of hundred steps or so Renaldo would say something to someone or acknowledge someone he knew and with whom he continued an on-going conversation.

A woman in her thirties came up and grabbed him by the arm and said, "Who is he?" indicating that Blake looks like a fine man to her.

Blake was wrapped up in what he and Renaldo were saying but his eyes continually moved here and there taking in the night sights of people on the street living their lives and swirling in all this energy. A thousand snap shots of these actions were in his head like the one of a hauntingly familiar guy looking straight at him from a poster on the side of a moving bus.

Not very many minutes later they came to Evan's building and Renaldo buzzed his number. A female voice came over the speaker saying Hello and Renaldo answered.

Renaldo: Hi, Jennifer, it's Renaldo and Blake.

There was a buzzing sound at the inner door. Renaldo pushed it open and they walked through. The entrance hallway of Evan's building was far from opulent but it was nice—wide and comfortably well lit. Most of all, there was a strong, spacious elevator. Blake was glad for this since it meant he didn't have to lug his backpack up four flights of stairs.

Jennifer met them in the hallway outside the elevator. She hugged Blake and began talking about how long it had been since she had seen him and how good it was to see him now. Blake, too, was very happy to see her after such a long time. Walking into the apartment she said,

Jennifer: What do you think of our coffee shop?

Blake: It's a very nice coffee shop and this is a great apartment, too. Evan told me the story about finding the coffee. It sounds like you guys have been having your share of adventures.

Jennifer: Yes. You know Evan—never a dull moment! You know, something I was thinking about today was that you have never met Claire. It's been that long since we've seen each other.

Blake: That's right. The only time I've seen Claire is in the pictures you send at Christmas. How old is she now?

Jennifer: She's eight years old now. She's quite a little lady.
Renaldo: So Blake has never met Claire. Wow, that's something. Claire's a really great little girl. Where is she?

Jennifer: She's in bed right now. She was already asleep when you called and said you were coming. She has school tomorrow, of course. Come on, I'll take you back there and you can look in on her while she's sleeping. I was telling her about you earlier today. She was full of questions such as how and where did we meet you and why has it been so long since we've seen you.

They walk down the hall to the door of Claire's room and Jennifer quietly opens it so they all can peek in. Blake takes a long look inside at the beautiful little sleeping girl and comes back out into the hall saying what a cutie she is.

Jennifer: How are your boys? You know it's been a long time since I've seen them too. In fact, I've only seen Randy one time and he was a little baby then. I'm sure he's grown up by now.

Blake: Yeah, he's almost eleven now. He's involved in a lot of things but mostly music. He's into playing the piano. And Robert is just getting into girls.

Renaldo: You've got two boys Blake?

Blake: Yeah I've got a house full of boys.

Renaldo: They keep things interesting, huh?

Blake: Yeah, pretty much.

Renaldo: Yeah, Claire is a live wire, too. She's very curious and she loves to read about all kinds of things.

Jennifer: She likes to know everything that's going on. Don't be surprised if she grills you about something. I told her you are a head doctor and she was interested in that. She asked me if that is the same thing as a shrink.

Blake: Yeah, what'd you tell her?

Jennifer: I told her yes. Of course she doesn't know what a shrink is either.

Blake: Well I guess I've got my work cut out for me. Will I see her in the morning?

Jennifer: Yeah, you'll probably see her before she goes to school but not for long. This is her week to ride to school with her friend Veronica and her mom from down on the third floor.

Blake: Oh, well, that's convenient.

Jennifer: Yeah, it really comes in handy. We trade off every other week. How are you feeling? Are you tired? If you are I can show you your room and help you get settled.

Blake: I'm not in a big hurry, but it has been a fairly tiring day.

Renaldo: Yeah, I know you're tired and I want to stop by a friend's house on the way home, so I think I'll take off and head that way.

    Renaldo starts making moves toward the door and they all move slowly back out into the foyer. He takes his leave saying good-bye to Blake and how glad he will be to see him tomorrow. They all agree he'll come by there in the morning. He'll call a few minutes before he arrives. They say good-bye to Renaldo and he leaves.

Blake: From the looks of the coffee shop tonight business is good.

Jennifer: Yeah, I think we're actually getting to be fairly well known, at least here in the neighborhood.

    Blake told her about the man he had run into when he came up from the subway tunnels and agreed about their getting known.
    Jennifer and Blake turn their conversation to some reminiscing about old times and checking on people they used to know in common but Blake was fading fast and soon he told her how glad he was going to be to get into the bed. She was very understanding and began showing him what he needed to know.
    They continue talking a little about her family and how she likes New York. Blake remembers about the notes he made for the questionnaire, trying to see if the drops put in the coffee facilitate realization. He took his pad out of his backpack and gave them to her. She said she would type them out on her computer and print a mock-up of what the questionnaire might look like. He thanked her and went into the guest room and closed the door. Within ten minutes he was fast asleep.

Chapter Four

The Evidence

Blake awoke at his normal time, a good bit before the sun came up. There was a dream floating on the river that carried him to that moment. With him were Evan and Renaldo and some people from the group, as well as Jennifer, his wife, Lacy, and a couple of other close friends.

They were wandering around in a county fair. Blake and Lacy's two boys, Robert and Randy, were there. So were Evan and Jennifer's little girl, Claire. There were other folks there but they were Blake's group were the only ones who knew each other well. They were very good friends. Blake felt that feeling of slipping from dream to being awake in a subtle, seamless transition.

It was his favorite time of day, the very first hours of the morning. It was meditation time, a time for going over things, pondering whatever comes through and being aware of being with God.

There were, of course, other things in his awareness—sounds from the street outside his window, particularly the cooing of some pigeons fairly close, and the random thoughts ambling through his head. He paid little attention to those, only paying attention to the ones that came forward, for whatever reason.

He had no need to get up. He wanted to put off getting up. He would do as he always did when sleeping in someone else's house. He would wait until he hears sounds outside his room that indicate someone else is awake.

In the meantime he would spend his favorite time in this favorite way. There were the events of yesterday. Lots of noticeable things were rolling through his mind.

Blake (in his private, inner self): What an amazing thing to be living on planet Earth, as a regular citizen of the universe when almost no one else on Earth knows anything about it.

Now is a great time to try to help fellow Earthlings wake up to the way the universe really is and what it's like. They really don't know the real world, do they? We're just like the people were in Copernicus' time. We're so self-centered; we have a very hard time learning and being aware of important things about the way the universe really works.

It's so exciting to try to shine a light on the classic egocentric stumbling block, The Copernican Error. I want to do all I can to lift the awareness of everyone on Earth to a realization that we are now, as we always have been, embroiled in The Copernican Error.

In this meditational mode, Blake is inside himself in a fully familiar way and place. It's a place of being awake and in a high quality state of awareness. It's like a big bubble of knowing his own internal self and what's going on there. He's in touch with whatever important things in his life might be passing through just then—his hopes, his dreams, his fears, his fantasies, his desires.

It is image/content shaped into words floating in a big, sizeless inner space. He's used to it. He knows it intimately. He comes here regularly. He does the familiar awareness actions that are not verbal.

He up-steps the awareness quality and expands to a simple emptiness that easily and objectively notices the important issues passing through. He's clear in his awareness of himself being there, with God.

Thoughts running through his mind are fewer and less frequent, less indentured and indenturing. He's in a timeless time immeasurable. Time is a thing known only as this and now—a broad, indefinite estimation because it obviously can't be measured and because he has no interest in that.

Matters of interest and great import fill his head while awareness of a large number of detailed meanings attached to the topics are in his mind at the same time: Evan's house and block, his neighborhood and the whole city, Evan and the coffee shop, the people in the shop, the people of Earth so fully entrenched in The Copernican Error, so oblivious to their mistakes and the true nature of the universe. Blake ponders the plans for today.

Blake (in his private, inner self): Today we're going to discuss the evidence for the idea that the real universe we live in is organized, populated, and governed by one central government. I can imagine what many of their issues will be.

There will likely be a strong energy resisting the idea. Their doubt will be the main thing pushing them. That's normal. People's doubt always leads them outside the pale when looking at something strange and unfamiliar. Most, if not all, of our time will be spent considering their first reactions after hearing about the book that gives us the information about the universe. They will be sounding out their negativity. They will be comfortably familiar with their doubt.

Many will feel it only reasonable and prudent to assume that such a book purporting to be authentic cannot possibly be real even though they probably won't be very clearly in touch with the unconscious assumption that makes them think this way.

"Why do you think that way about it?" I'll ask. Their answers will be along the lines of, "Because we've just come to believe that way through our experience with so many scams and people selling phantasmagoria that turns out to be trash. There are so many such bogus things in our world there's no way ANY of them—not even ONE—could be true. How gullible we would be to believe that the universe is truly this way."

The Copernican Error has a positive function at the deepest most primitive level—survival. It's the fundamental urge to be self-centered and protect one's self in its positive function. But in the higher levels of life it turns out to be dysfunctional. That's when we get to the things that are better done through cooperation and collaboration—seeing that we are not the center of reality.

The Copernican Error is the belief deeply ingrained in each of us that we are the center of everything. It is the fundamental drive to protect, strengthen, and further the interests of the home team. As such it's not an error. But it *is* the basic ego error.

It's a primary force in the basic functioning of everyone's inner spiritual/emotional/motivational deep unconscious mind and much of what it does is mess us up.

The Copernican Error is the original right and positive purpose of survival distorted in an erroneous direction. As ego it is fully selfish. It distorts, makes us competitive and argumentative, pits us against each other, makes us defensive and suspicious of each other, doubtful of what someone's telling us even if it's true, because we don't trust and we don't think well enough to distill down accurate truth on our own.

We are fools. We trust and depend upon the truth we have absorbed by osmosis from our culture. If the truth we are facing is outside the frameworks of our established culture we assume it's untrue without really taking the time to test it or analyze it in detail.

We are particularly fools because we don't recognize ourselves as fools. We don't just fall prey to this primary and "mother of all errors" error that is The Copernican Error, we also fall prey to all of the thousands of little daily errors that come from it.

We hate being wrong. It humiliates us. We feel inferior. We think we should be superior. Our ego is terribly offended when we're wrong so we deny that we're wrong when we really are, and we lose the opportunity to make ourselves right when we do this hiding from our errors.

Blake heard a knock at the door. He had been aware of little noises in the background of his thoughts for a little while now. There had been walking and rattling around in the kitchen and even some muffled sounds of people talking to each other. He had chosen to ignore them.

Blake: (Loudly) Hello, are you awake?

Evan: We've got some breakfast out here. Come on and have some coffee. (chuckle, chuckle)

Blake: Is it regular Maxwell House or some of that good stuff that REALLY wakes you up (sitting up and putting his feet on the floor)? I'll be right with you.

He stands, pulls on some pants and a favorite sweatshirt from his backpack, checks himself in a mirror hanging there, and goes out the door to breakfast. The kitchen is brightly lit, warm, harmoniously colorful, and very inviting to anyone who enters.

He immediately sees Claire sitting at the table. He had heard her talking out here.

Blake: Hello, you must be Claire.

Claire: Hi, are you Blake?

Blake: Yeah, it's me . . . from long, long ago and far away in the lives of your mom and dad.

Jennifer: He goes back to a time when we didn't know you. But we figured we'd be seeing you sometime soon.

Evan: (to Blake) Claire's heard about you quite a bit. So now (to Claire) you've seen him too, huh sweetie?

Claire: Yes I see him. There he is right there (laughing and pointing at Blake). Right there, right there. He's the man sitting right there. You used to know him and now I know him too.

Claire is smiling very big and pointing and wiggling her finger at Blake.

Claire: Are you really a head shrinker?

Blake: Oh, that's just a silly thing people say.

Claire: Why do they say that?

Blake: It's silly, isn't it? Of course I don't REALLY do that.

Evan: How about if, for now, we just say it's silly? We'll talk about it more some other time.

Evan: Hey, how'd you sleep Blake?

Jennifer: (musically) Yeah, good morning Blake. How long have you been awake?

She remembered that about him.

Blake: I'm feeling good and very rested. It's nice in that room, and what a nice kitchen this is!

He takes a chair at the table next to Evan. Evan gets up to pour some coffee.

Jennifer: Here have some coffee and a biscuit while I cook you some eggs. How do you want yours? Scrambled? You want yours fried (to Claire), right little girl?

Claire: Yes, please . . . little momma.

Blake: Sounds good. I have fond memories of great breakfasts in your house.

Blake watches Jennifer in a socially acceptable way admiring how pretty she is. She goes back over to the stove and cooks the eggs. At the same time she starts talking with Blake about his trip up from DC, how Lacy is doing, etc. Evan returns to his seat at the table and eats his last bite or so of eggs. Claire talks with her mom about something planned at school today.

Soon there is a little lull in the conversation.

Evan: I wouldn't want you to think I've forgotten that this morning you're going to tell me the evidence you have for this belief that the universe is populated, organized, and governed.

Claire (seeing it's becoming no longer her kind of conversation): I guess it's time for me to go to school.

Everyone says goodbye to Claire and Jennifer tells her something to tell Veronica's mom. Claire grabs her backpack and goes out into the foyer with Jennifer.

Blake: Well, it's really not a big secret or something very astonishing or anything. It's really very simple. I just didn't want to get into it yesterday when we were sitting there in the coffee shop. It's a lot better here at your place where it's quiet. There's no one here but you and Jennifer and Claire. Here we can have a relaxed and thorough conversation.

The evidence I'm talking about comes from a book . . . a very extraordinary book. It's written by non-humans and it was commissioned to be sent here by the highest authorities of the universe government. It was delivered through a very special connection. One of its purposes is to tell about the universe government. It also tells us in fair detail about a lot of other things.

There followed a fairly long silence with Evan looking at Blake and Jennifer (coming back from the foyer) mostly looking at Evan. She could see Evan was rattled . . . uncomfortable as though he had been told by someone like Chicken Little that the sky was falling. Jennifer could see she had missed something important.

Jennifer: What was the evidence?

Evan: Well, I have to say (stammering) I wasn't expecting a book. I hope it's not the book of some sect or something. I was hoping it would be a scientific study or something like that . . . at least an article by a respected astronomer.

Blake: Well, I knew there was a good chance you would have a hard time with it. I've always been amazed at how many people have a hard time with there being a book that tells us about the Universe Civilization. But, if you think about it you can see it's really quite good evidence and it's reasonable that, at the right time, they might send us a book. It may be the only evidence that is convincing.

After all, what about the Bible? Isn't it possible they could send us a new Bible? They sent us Jesus, didn't they?

Plus, it makes sense that a book like this would not have any Earthly agency proving it's true. It is its own proof and each of us must decide about it. It is important to see that the book itself is the major evidence for the Universe Civilization and it is also its own evidence.

By this time, Jennifer is looking directly at him and is clearly considering what he is saying. Evan also is over the initial shock and is giving what Blake is saying focused consideration.

Blake: The central and primary question of them all is whether or not the book is true. Is it really what it says it is? It says it is an official document sent here by the highest authorities of the Universe Civilization.

Is this so or not? The only way one can tell is to look squarely and thoroughly at the book itself and read it.

The writers of the book declare this. They say the only real way to authenticate the book is to read the book. There is no authority on Earth—not science, not a religion, not a committee, not a government, *nothing* that can pronounce it true or false. Each individual must come to his or her conclusion for himself or herself. The writers simply and unequivocally say that the real verification of the book is left completely up to the witness of God's spirit in the hearts of men and women.

If the book is what it says it is, then the news the book brings is true and to be depended upon. The book tells us in a fair amount of detail about the reality of the universe civilization—the Kingdom of Heaven that Jesus was talking about.

Evan: Well it's a little hard to know what to say. I can see you're right; the main issue has to do with whether the book is true . . . or real. How does one know that?

Blake: One has to settle down, go slow, spend some time, and get to know it. Things like this change over time as you get to know them and as you get deeper and digest them. I think it's something you have to be a little slow about. You have to spend some time when you can't be distracted and then you have to reflect a while on what you're reading.

You know how concentration varies from time to time. Sometimes you know you're concentrating better than at other times. There's no reason to be in a hurry. It's very important. It's something to take time with.

Evan: I can see that the issues are very big. I'm just realizing that if the book is real, then the basis of everything changes.

Blake: Right.

Evan: It means our American government is not the highest government and the background of lobbying and lying in politics, money grabbing, beating each other, and rich people running things and having wars to help their businesses is going to change *completely*.

Blake: This will happen when everyone realizes the realities of the book. If the book is not real then wow, it's really some kind of cruel joke and very sad—a killer of hope.

If the book is true, then when everyone realizes it the world will undergo a transformation of colossal proportions. Even if just a very large number of people realize it, there will be a lot of pressure for making things better.

Then there was a buzzing from the outside door of the apartment. Someone was downstairs on the street buzzing to be let in. Jennifer, who had been listening intently to the conversation, got up, went to the front foyer, and over to the speaker by the door. She pushed a button and asked who it was. It was Renaldo. She pushed the other button to release the door and told him to come on up.

As she returned to the kitchen she said, "What's the name of this book and where do we get it?"

Blake: Translated into English, the name of the book is, *The Earth Book*. You can get it pretty much anywhere. It hides in plain sight. No one seems to be very interested in it. You can actually read it online.

Evan: I wonder what Renaldo will say to the news that the main evidence is a book written by non-humans.

Blake: I have an idea he won't be very surprised.

Evan looked at him in a strange way. He had seen the apparent ease of communication and understanding between them at the coffee shop. He didn't think Renaldo would be very impressed by evidence being a book.

Jennifer: Well, I guess I'll go let him in (there's a knock at the door).

Jennifer walks into the foyer and opens the door. She and Renaldo exchange greetings and chat a bit as they move through the foyer and into the kitchen where Evan and Blake join in the conversation and greeting.

Renaldo is clearly quite excited. He is very happy to see everyone and seems particularly focusing on Blake.

Renaldo: Last night after I got home, I talked with my friends who showed me the book (he was looking at Blake). I asked them if they thought the universe is populated, organized, and governed. They quickly responded yes, it definitely is.

Evan (surprised): Oh, so you know about this book. I thought I was going to hand you a big surprise by telling you about it, like Blake told us this morning.

Jennifer: Where did you find out about it?

Renaldo: I have some friends who showed it to me a couple of months ago. I haven't really thought much about it or spent any time with it, though. I just put two and two together last night when Blake and I were walking over here.

Blake: I told him last night that the main evidence was a book. He asked me the name. I told him and he put things together from there. I wondered last night if you would call your friends (looking at Renaldo). I didn't know exactly how curious you were.

Renaldo: Yeah, I called them as soon as I got home last night. We talked in greater detail about the book and I told them about your showing up at the Coffee Shop yesterday.

They were very interested in the things you were talking about. They said they would try to come to the Coffee Shop this afternoon. They were particularly interested in the thing about the coffee and the realizations.

Jennifer: Who are these people?

Renaldo: They are friends I've known for a long time but we're not real close. I think I met them at a Rosicrucians' meeting a long time ago. It must be, uh, well, it must be more than fifteen years ago. I got very interested in the Rosicrucians back then but I didn't stick with them much. I met some really interesting people, though. They're a good group—very smart.

    Jimmy and his wife, Freda, are the ones I stopped to see a couple of months ago. I ran into them at a gathering in the park and went over to their house that evening. That's when they showed me the book. At the time, I didn't get very interested. But now I am. Last night when Blake and I were talking about the book, walking over here I realized I had probably seen it.

Evan: These friends of yours, what are they like?

Renaldo: I think you'll like them, Evan. They're very sane, normal, down-to-Earth people. They're not kooks. They're almost the opposite of that—very reasonable and very open and friendly. Jimmy is the one who's coming over to the shop today—Jimmy Handel.

Evan was quite off his game right now. The curve Blake had thrown about the book had blindsided him. He hadn't expected it. It set off a struggle inside him. One part of him was being very loud and insistently negative. That part was afraid Blake was essentially talking about some new scripture or the writings of some crazy kook who wasn't even very well known. Evan was very negative about this.

Evan (in his private, inner self): On the other hand, this is Blake—my friend for many years—a person I hold in the highest regard.

Evan was very surprised and nonplussed by Blake being involved with this book, apparently for a long time. Why had he never told him about it before?

If the book is big and important enough to tell us about this universe civilization, why had he never heard about it? Why had Blake never mentioned it to him? Perhaps it's because Blake knew he would respond just as he is right now. That was a disconcerting thought. He did not want that to be the case.

Evan did not want to be seen by Blake as unable to entertain new and unusual things. He pointed out to himself that he really is responding according to his predetermined notions about such books, before he even sees this book. He didn't want to do that, but he found it virtually impossible to keep from it. His negativity toward the book was very strong. Once again he learns something about himself from Blake.

Then an idea comes into Evan's mind that gives him some movement relative to this conflict. Of all the bogus books there are in the world like the ones he's suspicious of, could there be one—just one—that is true and authentic?

Evan (in his private, inner self): Surely the answer is *yes*. The question now is whether this one Blake is talking about is *the one*. If the unlikely event were to happen that he was going to run into that one genuine book, it makes sense that it would be associated with Blake.

Evan and Blake are each looking intently at one another. Then Evan tells Blake the essence of the thoughts just described, the struggle he's going through concerning the whole thing. He tells him how he doesn't want to let his prejudices distort his judgment, but it's basically impossible to control. He says he also has a prejudice that makes him want the book to be true, but that alternative scares him since it's such a colossal change and readjustment.

Blake: It's good that you see all these issues inside yourself. You are caught on the horns of several dilemmas. It's very understandable that these things would be so upsetting. It's all so new and you feel that you've been blindsided by reality, but you should have faith that this is going to all turn out okay and you'll make a good decision.

Remember, there's no hurry. Maybe you feel right now that there's reason to hurry. Maybe you feel you must make a decision right now. Maybe you feel there's a lot of pressure to go one way or another. I think that's all pressure you're putting on yourself. It's important to go slowly right now.

Evan: How long have you known about the book?

Blake: For quite a few years—almost ten.

Evan: You've known about it for ten years and you've never mentioned it to me? Of course, I know we haven't seen each other much over the last ten years.

Blake: And this is not the kind of thing you tell someone casually when you're having a phone conversation about something else or getting together for lunch on a rare and hurried one-day trip to New York.

Plus, since I became certain about the book myself, I've been steadily surprised by the way different people respond to it. I can never predict who's going to be amenable and who's not. Some of the most respected people I know are completely turned off to it and will not consider it.

You notice, however, I did share with you a major concept from the book a long time ago. At that time you seemed unreceptive but yesterday I found out that the concept had been rolling around in the back of your mind and it came popping up when you first drank the coffee with the drops.

Evan: Yes, that's interesting isn't it?

Jennifer: Oohh yeaaah. That *is* interesting, isn't it? So the idea you got from Blake back then about the universe being civilized and governed came from the book, and you—your mind—kept it alive inside you. Your mind brought it back up to you. I hadn't thought of that.

So if the notion of a civilized and governed universe is true, it speaks for the truth of the book. Now we have the book and the concept of a civilized universe being mutually supportive. The decision about whether the two of them are true is even more in focus now. My feeling or my guess is that they are true, but now I see there's work to do to study this decision further and make the whole business clearer. We have to look very carefully at this book.

Evan: What's the name of the book again? I just looked up "The Earth Book" on my laptop and that doesn't seem to be it.

Renaldo looks quickly and curiously at Blake as though to say, "What's this?"

Blake: The name of the book is *The Urantia Book*. Urantia is the name of this planet in the universe language.

Renaldo looked a bit relieved. It was surprising to him that Blake had called it "The Earth Book." He thought maybe Blake is a little too reticent to tell people about the book. He actually seems to avoid it.

Renaldo: Do you actually avoid telling people about the book sometimes, Blake?

Blake: Yes, at this stage in my experience with the book I do. I find people like concepts from the book a lot more than they like the book itself.

Evan: I just looked up "Urantia Book," and I ran into a long list of references. So I see *The Urantia Book* has quite a presence online.

Blake: Yes, there's quite a bit of stuff on the Internet about the book, but I would encourage you to spend your time with the actual book itself, not all the stuff people say about it. The entire book is on the Internet if you want to read it there for free. You won't have to buy it but I recommend that you do. Maybe you can read it online until you make up your mind about it. I can see how you wouldn't want to buy it if you don't think it's true.

Evan: I have to admit, I feel like a huge weight has been laid on my shoulders. Here I am, trying to get a new business started and raise my family and deal with New York and ya-da ya-da, and now here's this big book I have to get into and make a decision about. Oh no! It makes my head swim.

Blake: Whoa, cowboy. This doesn't have to be done tomorrow. This is what I mean when I talk about going slow. Really, there's no hurry. The world's not going to end.

Relax, take your time. Try to find an undecided position inside. That's okay. Get comfortable with being undecided for a while—a LONG time if need be.

Also, you know you don't have to read the entire book—all two thousand pages. And it certainly doesn't have to be done tomorrow. Just read in the book. Spend some time with it. Get to know it. Read about things you're interested in and things you feel you know about. You will decide about it in time, if you just keep an open mind and stay engaged with it. Don't just go on what somebody else says. Make a decision for yourself.

Jennifer: Oh yeah. We don't want this book thing to just be a source of more stress. That puts it completely in a negative category. Isn't it wild how we have a tendency to do this? I think it's just the American way. Go fast, right now, and get it done tomorrow. That's the American way. Blake is right. Let's slow down and let the answer to this thing come in its own time. We can be unsure and we can be that way for a long time if we need to.

Evan: Yeah, that's right. That's really hard for me. I'm so used to getting things done as fast as possible. I have to make myself slow down and relax and not worry. This is going to take discipline. That's really wild. I'm realizing.

Jennifer and Blake really laugh right here. All four of them look at each other with big understanding smiles.

Renaldo: There are a lot of people who won't read the book at all let alone read all of it. In fact, those people are in the majority. That's the way things are in America today. If it doesn't fit into a thirty-second sound bite or you can't get it all done and digested quickly, then forget about it. It will take a lot of time to get everyone in our society to see these things. I guess we're not really ready for it.

Blake: That's one of the odd things about *The Urantia Book.* It's a paradox. It's the most important book ever printed here. If everyone read it, believed it, and understood it—particularly our leaders—our nation and our entire world would quickly be vastly improved, yet it's okay if you don't read it. Your life will go on and you will not be condemned. The angels will continue to work with you as they always have. As a nation and a planet, we will keep moving slowly toward the future God wants for us, living more perfectly within His will.

Renaldo: What's a paradox?

Blake: The book is important but it's not important. That's a paradox. It'll be great for you if you read it and use it, but it's okay if you don't. Paradoxically the book is important but it's not.

Evan: Well, guess what? It's time to get moving. I need to get over to the shop. You guys are going with me, right?

Renaldo: I was thinking of walking over to Jimmy and Freda's house this morning. Are you going to drive over to your shop?

Evan: Yes I've gotten addicted to taking the car over there during the day. It's faster (he looks at everyone and smiles really big).

Jennifer: Or sometimes I take you over there and drop you off so I can use the car, and get myself somewhere faster (she chuckles). Aren't we the fast movers?

Renaldo: You're just trying to keep up. I guess you can sometimes paradoxically catch up by letting go and falling behind—let it catch up with you.

Everybody looks at Renaldo and breaks out laughing.

Jennifer: I like that idea of letting it catch up with me. If this book is true, that's what we'll be doing waiting for the others to catch up with us.

Evan and Jennifer have a car. They pay to house it in a parking garage around the corner and about two hundred feet down the street from the building where they live. Evan also has a parking space in the alley behind the coffee shop. He keeps a chain across it. He can drive the car between their apartment and the shop.

Having a car is a high value luxury in New York, but Renaldo is not used to riding. He was thinking of walking to his friends' house this morning and he was rather hoping Blake would go with him.

Evan: Okay. How about you, Blake?

Blake: It looks like a pretty nice day out there. I see some sun shining in the windows. I think I'll walk with Renaldo if he doesn't mind. I'll go and meet Jimmy and Freda. Is that okay with you, Renaldo?

Renaldo: Of course. I'll be glad for the company.

Evan: Okay. You guys walk and I'll see you when you get there.

Renaldo: We'll come over there a little later in the afternoon.

Jennifer: Evan, how about if I take you to the shop this morning and come back here and work on the questionnaire about the coffee with the drops that Blake wants us to start passing out. Then later, after Claire comes home, we'll come over there and bring the questionnaire.

Evan (looking grumpily at her): Okay, I guess so. Somebody will bring you home then later when you need to come.

Evan knows Jennifer wants to be at the shop this evening when all the regulars are hearing about the book.

He's grumpy about the extra car trips and trouble required to take her home but he knows it's just his being his selfish, controlling self. The positive side of him actually wants Jennifer to be in on the discussion tonight. She can help him hear more about it because he'll have to be distracted by work a lot. He's also always glad for Claire to come to the shop. She likes it and wants to come and he wants her to feel some ownership.

The day is beginning to get underway. Blake goes into the guest room to make his bed and order his belongings. He will be sleeping there again tonight, so it's just a matter of getting his things together and leaning his backpack against the wall.

He wants to take a shower, so he uses the towel and washcloth Jennifer had given him and goes to the bathroom. He makes himself clean and presentable, his favorite sweatshirt packed away. In the living room, Renaldo waits to go downstairs to the street.

Evan and Jennifer are heading for the garage to get the car. They all leave the apartment together riding the elevator down to the front door. When they reach the sidewalk, Evan and Jennifer go to the left, Blake and Renaldo to the right.

Chapter Five
Real-izing The Kingdom

It was indeed a nice morning in Manhattan. The sun was bright and clear. The sidewalk sang with its usual hustle-bustle made by people in their nice morning-in-Manhattan mood. Renaldo turned to Blake as they walked along, a big happy smile on his face. He stretched his arms both out and up and slowly savored a deep, deep breath.

Blake: It's a really nice morning and here we are in the middle of your neighborhood.

Renaldo: Yep, the quintessential American neighborhood. It's just maybe a few steps behind California.

Blake: Well, I don't know about that. But it's quintessential to you. That's all that matters.

Renaldo: Jimmy and Freda's house is just about four blocks over. You'll like them.

Renaldo is clearly being his usual ebullient self, maybe a bit more than usual. His dark, curly hair that never needs combing strikingly frames his pleasant, distinguished face with its thick, dark eyebrows and olive skin. Again he keeps seeing and responding to people he knows, saying hey to this one and something in Spanish to another. This continually goes on during the entire walk.

Blake flashes in his mind on beautiful things about the moment.

Blake (in his private, inner self): He's the quintessential individual in the quintessential neighborhood. What incredible opportunities I run into some times. Renaldo is so fascinating. He is awake, able to see, able to adjust and adapt himself honestly to real, changing scenarios. It's my great fortune to have met him and have the chance to get to know him.

Renaldo: Wow, I had to be beat over the head to wake up to The Urantia Book. I saw it a couple of months ago and I was amazed at that time. I knew it was something I wanted to look at more closely. But it got away from me. I just went on down the road and forgot about it. It's so easy to be asleep and sometimes so hard to wake up.

Blake: Yep, that is characteristic of the difference between "sleep" and "wakeful." Being asleep is easy. Waking up takes intention—much more energy and effort.

They were walking at a brisk pace toward Jimmy and Freda's house but there was so much going on around them, they were fully engaged. They could not allow themselves to miss it. There were people laughing, talking, working, carrying things from here to there, coming from outside to inside, and inside to outside. There were cars with noises rolling down the street, horns honking, brakes squealing, engines racing, and the constant, chugging hum of the city.

Far on the other side of Houston Street a man and a woman were arguing face-to-face. None of their noise could be heard above the rest of the sounds and their visuals were only one of many but Blake commented to Renaldo.

Blake: Look at those guys over there. I wonder which one is right . . . and how many times have they had this argument.

Renaldo: From what you taught me before, I'd say they're both right, right?

Blake (in his private, inner self): He's pretty quick.

Blake (aloud): Right.

They kept walking and seeing and talking and sensing and feeling the moment as they moved lightly east on Houston Street. At Elizabeth Street, Renaldo made a gesture with his arm that they should turn right. They did this and down the street about four or five houses on the right they came to Jimmy and Freda's place. It was a brownstone building with about five steps leading up to the stoop. Ornate iron railings surrounded the stoop and the sides of the steps. They went through the outer door, pushed on the buzzer and, when the inner door buzzed, they pushed it open. Renaldo led them up the steps to the third-floor apartment where Jimmy and Freda lived. They knocked, Jimmy opened, and they all said hello roughly in unison.

Renaldo: This is Blake. This is Jimmy. I'm glad to be the one to put you guys together.

Jimmy: Hello! Renaldo has said a lot of good things about you.

Renaldo: Is Freda at work?

Jimmy: Yes, she usually gets home around five. She said she would come down to the coffee shop then.

Renaldo: Jennifer, Evan's wife, one of the owners, is going there later today, too, so we'll all meet there.

Blake: So you're a reader of *The Urantia Book*. Do you have a reading group here?

Jimmy: Yes. Freda and I belong to a group that meets once a week. We probably make it about three quarters of the time.

Blake: You're the one who showed Renaldo *The Urantia Book.* When you really see *The Urantia Book* it changes everything.

Jimmy: Yes, that's true. It makes everything better.

Blake: How long have you been a reader?

Jimmy: About twenty years. I go for long periods without reading it much but the basic structure it provides is the foundation of my life. It is constantly influencing me.

Blake: I understand what you're saying. A part of that structure that Renaldo and Evan and Jennifer and I are very busy discussing and pondering today is the basic physical structure of the universe. We are talking about realizing that the universe is populated, organized, and governed. This is a notion the people in our culture generally reject.

Jimmy: Yes. It is commonly believed that the Earth is the only inhabited planet or at least there aren't very many others and we are the "special" one.

Blake: Right. All of us absorb from our culture a belief that we are the center of everything. I call it The Copernican Error. Because of our bias about being the center of everything, we miss the very important and positive truth about the universe we're living in—namely, The Kingdom of Heaven. It's the same mistake our people made in the time of Copernicus. We miss a very important truth about reality because of our self-centeredness.

Jimmy: Yes, we are living in The Kingdom of Heaven and we don't even know it. If we would learn it, everything would be different.

Blake: It's so refreshing that you see this.

Jimmy: Something I think about a lot is The Lord's Prayer. It's the model prayer that Jesus gave to His disciples. They were puzzled and uneasy about prayer, so they asked him how to pray. My guess is that Jesus knew that the real important thing about prayer is fellowship with God. What is said isn't very important but He knew they were uneasy so he gave them some words to say as a prayer. It is very interesting what He told them to say:

"Our Father who art in heaven; hallowed be thy name," which is a statement of praise and worship.

Then notice what He says next: "Thy kingdom come, thy will be done on Earth as it is in Heaven." He has them pray for the coming of the Kingdom on Earth. So all of these years we have been praying for the coming of the Kingdom but we don't know what we're specifically praying for. We have these strange, unreal notions about Heaven. We think it's some strange never-never land off someplace else—not in the sky, the same sky the Earth is in. But the truth is the sky—that sky—is Heaven. Our planet is right in the middle of it. When all of us someday realize this and truly embrace it in our hearts, then will be the coming of the Kingdom of Heaven on Earth. We will all be full of joy to acknowledge that the government of The Kingdom of Heaven as our true government for our entire planet.

Blake: Boy! You said that so well. It's true. Every time we say the Lord's Prayer, we're praying for the coming of the

Kingdom and it might be true that every time we pray the Prayer the Kingdom comes a little closer.

I know that Jesus talked a lot about The Kingdom of Heaven and the thing He focused upon most was a now concept. He said we could find our own part in the Kingdom *now* in our hearts. In other words, we find our part in the Kingdom when we get our hearts right.

But Jesus also talked at times about the fact that sometime in the future, the Kingdom will actually come to be our established government here on Earth.

Your point is fascinating because what you're saying is that this will happen when we as inhabitants of Earth come to realize that the universal government does, in fact, exist. It is real.

Renaldo: Wow! What an incredibly fascinating idea! You're saying that as the people of Earth realize the reality of the universe civilization, they bring about the coming of The Kingdom of Heaven on Earth.

So, if we work now to help people wake up to the reality of the universe civilization, we actually work to bring about the coming of The Kingdom of Heaven on Earth. This means that what we are working on right there in Evan's Coffee Shop is furthering the coming of the Kingdom because we're giving people who drink the coffee an ingredient that helps them wake up. Then we're focusing their attention on whether the universe is populated, organized, and governed, which helps them realize the truth about The Kingdom of Heaven. It's real in the physical world and it's now, right here in the present.

Jimmy: When I think about how long it will take for those who see the authenticity of the book to reach a "critical mass" (making a gesture indicating quotation marks), I become easily disheartened. I guess I'm impatient or my mind just can't accurately grasp the scope and details of the process involved. People don't just have to be convinced of the physical realities of the universe civilization, but they also have to see the spiritual realities—the real nature of the values and culture of the universe civilization society.

Blake: I know what you mean. It's hard to be patient and trust in the inevitability of God's positive plan. We're all so small compared to the scope and magnitude of the system and we see so little of the details.

Renaldo: Learning all that is what real spiritual maturity is about, isn't it?

The three men continued on in this free associative conversation for a long time. Blake and Renaldo had left Evan and Jennifer's house a little after 11:00 in the morning.

During their conversation Jimmy went into the kitchen and came back with a chunk of cheese, some pickles, a bowl of tabouleh, and a plate of crackers. He asked if anyone wanted a beer and Blake said yes. Renaldo went with him to the kitchen and came back with a glass of ice water for himself. Jimmy had two beers—one for Blake and one for him. The fondness growing between them was very much noticed by Blake.

Blake (in his private, inner self): Jimmy is smart and a very gentle soul, Blake thought I'd say he and Renaldo are going to be much closer after today. Close to me, too.

They talked about the Coffee Shop and the sandwiches there and what could be done to augment the menu and make the place more of an attraction. They talked about a lot of things. They talked about the reality of Jesus and where He came from—The Kingdom of Heaven? They wondered about Jesus' Kingdom of Heaven—isn't it the same thing as God's creation? How real is that?

They talked about the current daily news and news that was a little less current. They talked about America and all of its issues. They talked about Americans being crazy about guns. They talked about politics and the corporate government. They talked about Christianity and technology and where everything is headed. They talked about sports and movies and the process of waking up. They talked about The Copernican Error and the fact that so many errors come from it.

As they talked, each became more in tune with the others. They became more and more focused on the conversation going on between them. They grew increasingly familiar with each other. Each was greatly enjoying this fine day in Manhattan and the topics that were open and alive between them—the process of realization, the populated, organized, and governed universe, the new coffee house and the coffee that may be facilitating realization.

Then Jimmy looked at the clock on his wall.

Jimmy: Hey guys, it's getting pretty close to 4:00 o'clock. Should we be heading toward the Coffee Shop?

Renaldo: Yeah, I'd say now would be a good time to start moving there. What do you think, Blake?

Blake: Yeah, that sounds right to me. You're going to take a Urantia book with you, aren't you Jimmy?

Jimmy: Yes, Renaldo says there are a lot of people there who are going to want to see it.

The three of them started getting up, moving around, and straightening their clothes and looking at themselves in the mirror, the way people do when they're preparing to walk from one location to another. Jimmy did these things in particular since it's his house and he has to get his pocket stuff including keys and put away things in the kitchen and straighten here and there.

On the surface, while this was going on, they continued the conversation, though perhaps it became a bit lighter. As they left the apartment, went downstairs, out onto the sidewalk, and started walking, they were joking about The Copernican Error. Blake had defined The Copernican Error as the belief that each person is the center of everything.

Someone said it was an error to think they needed to be at the coffee shop at a certain time or they would be missed.

Renaldo: Since I'm the center of everything, nothing important will happen before I get there.

Jimmy: I'm not just the center of everything, I'm the center of everything beyond that!

Blake: Since everybody is the center of everything, aren't they going to be running into each other a lot?

Renaldo: Well, that does happen a lot, doesn't it?

Jimmy: Just think all of these people down here on the street are at the center of everything. Everybody in the whole city is at the center of everything.

Blake: Wow, everything sure is crowded at the center.

Renaldo: No wonder people have such a hard time getting along.

They are busy with comments and little quips as they walk along. They're an interesting group to see—all very different but obviously comfortable and glad to be together. Jimmy is smaller than the other two, bald on top of his head and brown hair on the sides. Blake and Renaldo are close to the same height—around six feet give or take an inch or two. Blake has thick, short, sandy hair and very white skin. Renaldo is much darker with thicker, curly very dark hair, broad shoulders, and light on his feet. They're an interesting group but no one notices—*everybody's* interesting on the Lower East Side.

They're walking at an easy pace, not slow but not fast. Their conversation continues, but now it is peppered with comments about things encountered on the street. It doesn't take them long to come to the block on Bowery Street where the Starlight Café and Coffee Shop is alive with business, and within a few moments they are walking through the door.

Of the group of regulars, the ones who are already there are Carlene, Monet, Maggie, Liz, Lester, and Grolley. They all brighten up with obvious interest when they see the three, led by Renaldo, come through the door. Renaldo immediately engages with them and begins introducing Jimmy.

Blake (in his private, inner self): Gosh, I don't remember their names. This is one of my worst characteristics. How can a psychologist be as bad as I am at remembering names? There's Carlene, I remember her name; she's the only one whose name I remember.

Lester: Hi Blake. It's good to see you. For some reason I thought you'd be here all day today.

Blake: Does that mean you've been waiting here for a long time?

Lester: Well, no, not really. I've been here about a half hour. I just thought you'd be here when I got here. I was mostly eager to talk about the evidence we mentioned last night.

Carlene: Yes, me too. What about it? Are you going to tell us about evidence?

Alicia: Yeah, I want to hear, too.

Liz: Me, too.

Blake: Well, you know, I told Evan about it this morning and I think he was a little disappointed. Maybe you will be, too.

Josie: Really? Why was he disappointed?

Blake: It's basically because the evidence is a book.

Grolley: A book? What book? You mean the evidence is in the book?

Isabelle: Oh yeah? That is rather disappointing. Is it a study reported in the book?

Blake: Wow, you guys are really going fast. Listen (he begins to slow down), how about if we stop for a second and take a deep breath. Okay?

Renaldo: Yeah (speaking calmly and slowly like Blake). How about if we all not talk right now and let Blake talk a little while and give us an introduction to this evidence thing?

Michael: You mean, how about if we all wake up right now and pay attention to ourselves and what's going on in this moment and let Blake speak to us.

Monet: Aw, man . . .

Audrey (sarcastically): Well, thank you very much, Michael. Aren't you the teacher's pet? (A few chuckles rumble up from the group.)

Dede: C'mon Audrey, be cool.

Paco: Yeah, let's let Blake speak.

Gary: Okay, yeah let's let him speak.

Blake (having stayed quiet and calm until they really did get quiet): Thanks, I understand your excitement and impatience. You're right, this *is* a pretty big thing. Just think a second about the question we're ultimately dealing with. Is the universe populated, organized, and governed? If we say it's true but it's not, that's a big thing. And if we say it's not true and it is, that's also a big thing.

Let's go back to Grolley's question a little bit ago. He said, "What do you mean a book? You mean the evidence is in a book?"

The answer to that is yes, the evidence is in the book. But the evidence is also the book. That's because the book itself is a very unusual book. It is unlike any other book on Earth. Humans did not write it. It was commissioned and sent here from the highest authorities of the universe government.

The book tells about the universe and its structure and its government. It also tells a lot about many other things. It tells about the history of our planet and the history of the human race.

When you read it, you see what it's like. It does not say any silly things. It's obviously written by very intelligent beings and it is obviously telling a lot of very profound truths.

The name of the book is *The Urantia Book*. Urantia is the name of our planet in the universe language. We have a copy of it here with us tonight. It belongs to Jimmy who is a friend of Renaldo's and is sitting over there at that table. (Jimmy raises his hand.) Many of you met him when we first came in.

There was a short silence when Blake stopped talking. Then people started asking questions. Gary asked how long Blake has been reading it. Isabelle asked what makes Blake think it's not a hoax. Liz asked who publishes it, and Josie asked how many pages it has.

Blake started talking again.

Blake (speaking somewhat loudly): Listen, pay attention to me now because I'd like to focus on what I think is the main issue of all.

Everyone got quiet.

Blake: The key question is whether the book is true or not. This is the most important issue of all. Each person must decide. If *The Urantia Book* is true, then it is what it says it is. It claims to be the "Fifth Epochal Revelation" sent to our planet from the universe civilization. It says that Jesus was the fourth revelation sent here from the universe and it gives us much more detail about Jesus.

If the book is not true, then it is a very clever and extensive pack of lies and we don't know where they come from or who is responsible for sending them.

There is no earthly litmus test we can use to tell if it's true or not. It does not place itself under any earthly authority other than the witness of the spirit of God in the hearts of mankind. Each human must decide on his or her own about whether *The Urantia Book* is true.

I say the only honest and sensible way to make this decision for one's self is to expose one's self to the book. If you decide without reading the book that it is false, you are not deciding about the book. You are deciding on the basis of your preconceived belief that books that fit this profile or fall into this category cannot possibly be true. You are saying that within the laws of the universe, as you understand them, such a book is an impossibility.

Now understand me. I am not saying you must read the book cover to cover or word for word. No. I don't believe that's necessary. The thing to do is go slow and just read the book as your interests lead you. Spend time with it. Get to know it. There is a good bit of the book that we can't understand very well, but that's okay. We shouldn't worry about that. There's plenty of stuff we do understand and a whole lot of stuff that is extremely interesting and very inspiring.

Let me stop talking now. Let's go into a discussion time and let you talk or ask questions. Jimmy has the book over there. You can look at it. I want to encourage you to buy a copy of the book and don't be in a hurry. Just settle down to reading it little by little. Don't feel rushed. This is a very important decision and it's good to know yourself well as you read it and work on the decision. If you can't buy it now or don't want to, you can read it online for free. The whole book is there to read. But I do want to encourage you to not get distracted by what everybody else is saying about it. Try to make your own decision. Let me sit down and be quiet.

Blake (in his private, inner self): Boy, what a spew that was. I wonder what they got out of it. You never can tell with The Urantia Book. People are always so filled with wild and different notions—strange theories from God knows where.

While he was still talking, Blake saw a woman come in and sit down with Jimmy. She had what looked like a Urantia book under her arm. He figured it must be Freda, home from work. Several people are coming to stand around Blake and want to talk.

Michael: Blake, you're really convinced that the book is true. What's the main thing that makes you so certain?

Blake: Well, there are a number of things. First off, everything I read in *The Urantia Book* just has the ring of truth about it. The things the book says are reasonable and sensible.

Secondly, the book is completely consistent within itself. If it's fake, then some human or some group of humans wrote it and we have no hint about who they are or why they wrote it.

I really can't believe any human or group of humans could make that whole thing up and have it be as clear, detailed, elaborate, and as internally consistent as the book is. Art and imagination can imitate reality, but they never do as good a job as reality itself. *The Urantia Book* is just obviously very real.

Thirdly, you could say it was written by the devil "the great deceiver" and maybe that could be, but why would the devil give us a book that tells us on the one hand frankly and straightforwardly about him (the devil) and who he is and how he became the devil and then, on the other hand, give us the rest of the book that is so totally positive and redemptive?

Fourthly (and there are even more reasons than this, but let's hold it here), I've been reading the book for many years and I've been hanging out with other readers all that time and nobody has ever come up with anything they read that made them doubt the authenticity of the book. Very much to the contrary, everything points to the alternative, that it is true.

People are milling around now. Several have heard what Blake just said and now they are talking in little groups and going over to Jimmy and Freda, looking at the book.

One listening could hear a lot of opinions. Some people are puzzled that they ever got involved in this business about the universe. Others are very intrigued. Some see the importance of the whole thing, then, contradictorily they don't—they wonder what all the fuss is about.

Blake is an interesting guy and, for a while, his question about whether the universe is populated, organized, and governed held their attention but now there's a huge two-thousand-page book involved and they wonder if he's just selling some new religion.

People are still talking to Blake. He's talking about *The Urantia Book,* the universe, and/or the process of realization. The little coffee shop is filling with people when Jennifer comes in with Claire. Blake sees her come in and begins to bring his conversations to a close and make his way over to where she and Claire and Evan are standing by the door that goes to the employees' area.

Blake: Hey, hello. I see you made it. Hi, Claire, how are you?

Claire: Hi.

Jennifer: Yeah, here again. One more time. Here's the questionnaire.

Jennifer hands him the mock-up of the questionnaire that she laid out on her computer. He takes it and looks it over. It looks like this:

> # Starlight Café and Coffee Shop Questionnaire
>
> Date _____
>
> A recent popular theory says the universe is fully populated, organized, and governed by a central government.
>
> What is your opinion? Do you agree?
>
> _____ Yes, I believe it is true.
>
> _____ It is possible and it probably is true.
>
> _____ It is possible but probably is not true.
>
> _____ No, I believe it is not true.
>
> Is this your first visit to the New Coffee Shop?
> Yes _____ No _____
>
> If No, how many times have you been here before?
> _____
>
> Are you drinking the house coffee with the drops added?

Blake: Thanks Jennifer. This looks pretty good.

Evan: Yeah, I thought so, too. As soon as you give your approval, we'll start handing it out.

Blake: Let me look at it a little more closely tonight, okay?

Evan: Okay, that's good. So now here we are; we're all here. How did they take the idea about the book?

Blake: Well, I can't really tell. It'll take a while but I think I see something happening that I see often. People who were at first very interested in the question about the universe have now cooled off to that question because they see there's a big book involved. It's amazing how phobic people are of big books. I think they probably prefer Harlequin novels.

Jennifer: Yeah, that's funny. I can see that now, too. I never thought of it before.

Evan: Come on, let's go over to the regulars' corner and I'll introduce you to Jimmy and I guess it's his wife.

Blake: Yes, I assume that's Freda. She's also a reader.

They walk the ten or so feet over to the "regulars' corner" and Renaldo stands up. Things get a little quiet for a bit and everybody is introduced to Jennifer and Claire and Freda. Many already know Jennifer and Claire but they are glad to have a formal introduction.

Carlene: Hello! It's good to formally meet you guys. Jennifer, of course we know you from seeing you around, but it's good to get an introduction. My name is Carlene.

Jennifer: Hi, yes it is good to be introduced and to connect some names to some faces.

Maggie: Hi, I'm Maggie. We really like your coffee shop here. There's never a dull moment. What do you think about this book and this business about the universe?

Jennifer: Well, I vote yes on the universe thing. It just makes so much sense to me. It seems so much more likely that the universe is full and organized as Blake says than cold, dark, and empty as we have thought. It especially seems so very much more likely if you want to unite your belief about God with your experience with the rest of reality. By the way, this is my little girl, Claire.

The ones (mostly women) standing around this conversation say hello and pay a good deal of attention to Claire. At the same time they tell Jennifer that they agree with her and that what she's saying makes a lot of sense. Blake was listening to this conversation and rubbing Claire on the top of the head.

Blake: Yes, I agree that what Jennifer just said makes a lot of sense. If people wake up and pay attention to uniting their belief in God with their experience of reality (God's creation), it makes a lot of sense that the rest of God's universe would be as fully developed and elaborate as our planet Earth is. And it makes sense that they might send us a book like *The Urantia Book*.

Winfry: I've been talking with Jimmy and Freda and they say there's a group of readers here on the Lower East Side who have been meeting and reading on a weekly basis for a long time. It seems to me that might be one of the best ways to get to know the book and make a good, informed decision about it.

Jimmy: Yes, this group is open to anyone who wants to come and read along.

Freda: The group usually meets on Thursday nights at one of several different places. Anytime you want to come you can just call us. We can tell you where it's meeting that night and we can give you the phone number to call. Our phone number is 212-749-8103. Feel free to call us anytime.

Blake: I hope you get to know Jimmy and Freda. Renaldo and I spent the whole day today with Jimmy and it was a very enjoyable day. One of the things Jimmy said today is standing out in my mind.

Jimmy pointed out what was mentioned in the model prayer Jesus gave His disciples. They asked Him to give them a prayer. I guess they were uneasy about prayer. I would say they were waking up to the whole idea of prayer and they discovered they knew very little about it. They asked Jesus what they should pray about and He gave them an interesting prayer. He suggested it to them as a model they could use, but Christians have not been using it as a *model*; they've been praying it verbatim for a couple of thousand years.

Jesus said to try this. First He opened with a statement of respect and praise, "Our Father who art in heaven, hallowed be thy name." Then He suggested they say this fascinating, thing: "Thy Kingdom come, Thy will be done on Earth as it is in Heaven." He was having them pray that Earth would be fully, formally, and intentionally brought into the precincts of the Heavenly Kingdom where God's will is done in a much more perfect way.

Then He goes on and suggests that they pray for their needs to be met—"Give us this day our daily bread"—and learn about forgiveness as well as get help dealing with temptation and evil: "Forgive us our debts as we forgive our debtors and lead us away from temptation and evil." Then again He mentions the Kingdom: "For Thine is the Kingdom, the power, and the glory forever. Amen."

So here, if we really wake up and realize what is happening, we will see that Jesus set this up so that for hundreds of years we would all be praying as a group for God's Kingdom to come on Earth.

And it turns out that what we've been doing right here in Evan and Jennifer's coffee shop for the last little bit is also toward that end—the coming of the Kingdom. Tonight, when we realize what's going on, we recognize that the coming of the Kingdom on Earth is really just a simple matter of us humans realizing that it exists and we are already a part of it.

Alicia: Wow, that is an amazing thing. I've never thought of it that way until just now. Have any of the rest of you ever thought about that?

Lester: No, I haven't. It is really interesting.

Katherine: Yes, it's fascinating. People have been praying for it for hundreds of years and didn't realize what they were praying for.

Audrey: And what we were praying for is far greater than we ever imagined.

Grolley: "Thy Kingdom come. Thy will be done"—and it's not about something God does. It's about something we do. All we have to do is realize.

Everybody started milling around again only this time their energy was higher. They were moving faster and they were talking louder. They were getting pretty excited. Blake and Evan and Jennifer, Renaldo, Jimmy, and Freda all pulled into a group and had a little discussion. It was all fairly understood by Jennifer and Evan now that the book is a part of all of this and they just have to start including it in their lives in an easy, ongoing way just like Blake, Renaldo, Jimmy, and Freda have done.

As they were talking, Freda saw how interested Evan and Jennifer were, particularly Jennifer, and she offered to let them borrow her book for a while until they had a chance to buy their own.

Jennifer was very happy and excited about this. She and Freda got into a little conversation on the side where Freda sat down and showed her the basic layout of the book. Jennifer thanked her very much in a very sincere way and took Freda's book.

Then she turned her attention to the topic of Claire and her bedtime. Evan quickly said he'd run Jennifer, Claire, and Blake back to their apartment and come back to close things up. They said good-bye to Jimmy and Freda as well as quite a few others. They made plans with Renaldo for him to come by the apartment again in the morning to go shopping with Blake and Jennifer and run a couple of errands. Blake very much wanted to go to Saks Fifth Avenue to shop for a birthday present for Lacy. He has discussed this with Jennifer previously.

With that, the four of them leave and drive to Evan, Jennifer, and Claire's apartment. Evan drops them off and returns to the coffee shop. Jennifer, Claire, and Blake go up to the apartment and slowly go to bed.

Chapter Six

Lacy's Gift

The next morning, Blake wakes as usual before the Sun comes up. It's one of those easy, soft poppin' wake-ups that happen most of the time. You're in a dream and then, pop, you're awake. Slowly your mind starts bringing in all the business it knows is on the agenda for that day.

Blake (in his private, inner self): Hey, hello. Here we are again. We're going shopping today at Saks. That'll be fun. I feel you there, Father. I feel the endless bottomlessness of who you are and the authentic familiarity of us. I'm not very much on track with you as I do intend to be, but I'm yours. May I be more that way. I want to be more that way. We have to decide about the questionnaire. I had a thought last night about an addition and a change. I can't remember it.

He gets up, pulls on clothes, and goes out just after he hears noises outside his room. He doesn't wait for them to come to his door and call as he did yesterday. He finds all three in the kitchen again eating breakfast. This time they're eating cereal.

Blake: Good morning; how is everybody?

He pulls back a chair at the table, grabs a bowl and a box of cereal, and helps himself to breakfast.

Claire is talking with her mom about Veronica and what her mom said in the car yesterday. Jennifer gives her a message to tell her mom again this morning and then she starts chatting with Blake and Evan about today's agenda.

Blake (in his private, inner self): I remember what it was, Blake thinks. We should add to the questionnaire a question about whether they have had food and how much. The how much part probably needs some attention.

Basically, Jennifer's chatting about how she and Blake and Renaldo are taking the car up to midtown this morning so Jennifer can pick up some boots she had work done on and then they'll go to Saks so Blake can shop for a birthday present for Lacy.

Blake: I was thinking about the questionnaire and thinking we should add an item about whether they usually eat food with their coffee and if so is it a full meal or just a snack.

Jennifer: Okay, I see what you mean. I'll take care of that.

Blake: Thanks. Otherwise I think the questionnaire looks good. We don't want to make it too big.

Jennifer: Wow, I can't believe yesterday. We got started with all of that business about the book and it was a completely weird and wild idea to me. Now, one day later, I feel as though I've known the book for years and its existence is completely logical and old hat. What an eventful day yesterday was.

Somehow the whole notion that we, here on Earth, are just one little planet full of people set within the context of a vast universal civilization is breaking through to me more and more. It makes a lot of sense and it would make a lot more sense to everyone if it weren't for our Copernican Error. I'm also seeing what you mean by realization. The whole business has just become more intensely real to me in just the last few hours.

Evan: Yeah, I think it's sort of that way for me too. It's amazing how you can all of a sudden wake up to something and then look back and feel amazed again that you had been so asleep to it. That's how I feel. Of course, I think these feelings are particularly intense in this situation because the thing I'm realizing is so big. It's so monumental yet so very basic.

Now a call comes in on Evan's phone. He gets up and walks into the bedroom to answer. He can be heard talking on the phone from the kitchen but no one can make out what he's saying. That is, no one could hear him if they wanted to but, in fact, no one wants to. Blake, Jennifer, and Claire continue the conversation and in a few minutes Claire says good-bye and goes off downstairs to Veronica's house for her ride to school.

About now there's a buzz from the downstairs front door. Jennifer goes into the foyer and speaks with Renaldo on the intercom. He responds and she pushes the button to release the downstairs door. She leaves the apartment door ajar so Renaldo can come in when he gets there. She goes back into the kitchen.

Jennifer: Blake, do you have an idea about what you want to get for Lacy's Birthday present, or will just anything from Saks do?

Blake notices her comment about "just anything." He knows it's just one of those ideas about generalities women make regarding men, just like the generalities men make about women.

Blake: As a matter of fact, I was thinking about something done in colorful handmade ceramics—maybe a bracelet or a necklace.

Jennifer: I know just the place to go at Saks.

Blake: Well, Jennifer I'll just follow you then. I want to go to Saks so I can say it came from the New York store but I have no idea where in the store I should go. I just figured I'd follow my nose and ask people. Turns out I'll have a guide right there with me!

Jennifer: Is there any other place you want to go? We'll take Evan to the coffee shop and go on up there after we get ready here this morning. I think Renaldo's going too.

About this time, Renaldo walks in. He and Evan enter the room at the same time. They shake hands and pat each other on the shoulder and everyone greets Renaldo.

Evan: So, you guys are going shopping?

Jennifer: Blake wants to go to Saks downtown. I have to go up to midtown to the shoe repair shop where I left my boots last week. I thought we would drop you off at the coffee shop and run uptown, then come back when we're finished. Renaldo is going with us.

Renaldo: Yeah, I'm just along for the ride. I don't really have a plan for the day other than to meet with the others this evening at the coffee shop. I don't get up to Midtown much. I'd like to check and see that it's still there.

Evan: That sounds fine with me. I'd say it would take an hour or so for us to get ready to leave here. You guys would probably be pretty bored if you go with me this morning. I would like the ride, though. That was Tim on the phone and he needs to run an errand himself about 11:00.

Jennifer: Okay, that sounds good. We'll all take you there when we leave. I have to make a little change in the questionnaire. I'll do that while you and Blake get ready. I'll take the disk with us so we can stop in at a FedEx store while we're out and print some copies.

Blake: Thanks, Jennifer. This looks good. We'll get some copies made today.

   Renaldo was happy to have a little excursion like the one they were having today. Blake, too, was happy that he got just the opportunity he was hoping for. He's always impressed by Jennifer and how in tune she is with details of situations. He admires this.

Now he goes off to take a shower and get ready for the shopping trip. He's thinking about how much this little group has pulled together in a day. He agrees with Jennifer that a lot has happened in a day and everything feels a lot different compared to yesterday. This project of introducing *The Urantia Book* and getting everyone to start thinking about whether the universe is populated and organized has gotten off to a good start.

Blake (in his private, inner self): These people really have been very open. They responded positively to both the question about *The Urantia Book* and the question about the universe. It's rather amazing that there has been so much positivity.

He takes care of ordering his room and setting things up for him to return to them again tonight and he goes out into the living room.

Soon Evan comes and asks if Blake wants to go with him down the street to get the car. Blake says yes and they start toward the door discussing plan details with Jennifer and Renaldo as they go.

Everyone is busy with personal arranging and organizing. Evan and Blake head downstairs to the street. Renaldo and Jennifer stay behind to finish in time to meet them with the car in front of the building.

Renaldo is still feeling happy and excited. As he and Jennifer join Evan and Blake in the car, he's being a bit talkative and slightly elated. The others notice but it's okay.

Blake is spinning theories about what might be making him so positive. His main theory is that Renaldo's new realizations about *The Urantia Book* are continuing to register in his thoughts and he is very happy about what he thinks are the realities of the book—the real Kingdom of Heaven. The fact that there might really be beings and forces in his life that are deeply good and wise and powerful and that he can depend on.

Blake (in the car): You seem pretty up today, Renaldo.

Renaldo: Well, I hadn't thought about that but I guess you're right. I guess I am pretty excited. You know this Urantia concept is completely new to me and, when I think about it, I keep realizing that if it's true it changes everything. It changes the background of everything in my life.

I don't know, I'm just going through my day and all of a sudden it comes up in my mind. I get a very positive and peaceful and joyful feeling. The reality of the book and the universe Kingdom keep coming into my mind again and again.

I think about the book and the realizations keep coming up. They keep expanding. It gives me great comfort. I realize it's probably true. I figure there's no way we can know for sure if it's true or not, but if you just go with the probabilities, it seems most likely that it is true. That really excites me. If it's true and there is an ancient universe civilization, it makes sense they might send a book here.

Jennifer: Gosh, Renaldo, that's really interesting thinking. I agree with all of it. The book is a new thing for me too and I think it's probably true, but I think we need to read the thing. I believe if it's not true I'll be able to see that when I read it.

Evan: It sounds to me as though you guys are getting a little ahead of yourselves. You really do need to read it and I think you ought to suspend judgment until you do.

Renaldo: Oh, I agree with you there. I am suspending final judgment, but I'm also going over the logic that might apply if it's either true or not true.

Blake: I don't want to sound like I'm beating a dead horse, but I think I'm hearing a lot of realization going on here. You seem to be realizing what it might mean if the book is true. If it's not true, it doesn't mean that much. It only means there's a big pack of lies being published by somebody who gives us no clue as to who he or she might be or what the agenda is. Whatever the agenda, the author or authors are telling us some very positive stuff and a pack of lies that sound very true. If these people are spreading a bunch of lies, what is their purpose and why are their lies so positive and comforting?

Jennifer: Yeah, a big pack of lies is usually not so positive and they don't usually have such a ring of truth. If they are lies, they are for some strange, unknown reason.

A silence took over in the car at this point—a moment when each person turned to personal thoughts alone.

When they looked up, Evan had driven them into the alley behind the coffee shop. He and Jennifer got out saying goodbye and kissing. He moved toward the door. Jennifer got into the driver seat and drove back out toward the traffic.

She moved out, merging into traffic. They could all feel the claustrophobic sensation of being in a crowded Manhattan traffic flow as though they were in a little capsule riding through the veins of a big city monster. Everywhere they looked buildings were crammed together, there were power poles, light poles, concrete, and glass. There were sidewalks loaded with walking feet, little brown birds, bike messengers, maintenance men, construction workers, strange oddities, and trash that all seemed to run all over, up and down and around the corners.

Renaldo: Look at that.

An old, white, recycled church van was rolling along next to them. Blake, from his position in the passenger seat, looked over and saw several characters with big round googly eyes and long accordion hoses hanging from their noses with a brown canister at the end. It was a van carrying people wearing old gas masks. When it slowly passed he could see their license plate showing that they were from Tennessee.

The three adventurous friends lightly chatter about sights they see and thoughts they have, continuing in their happy mood.

Jennifer: What a beautiful day.

Blake: Yeah, the sky is really clear and the Sun is bright.

Renaldo: That's funny. I'm not very used to hearing people say things like that in Manhattan. It's as though the city is so dense and full of itself, you don't notice what the day is like.

The boot shop where Jennifer is going to pick up her boots was about three blocks east of Fifth Avenue, on 53rd Street. She drove up Fifth Avenue, passing Saks on the way so they could see where they were going next. Then she turned right on 53rd Street and made her way over to get her boots.

As luck would have it, there was a parking spot on the curb just about five or six car lengths from the boot shop. A truck had stopped in front of the boot shop. Its lights were flashing and the men from the truck were loading a couple of dollies with boxes of boots, bringing them into the store.

Just beyond the door to the shop, a Salvation Army volunteer was ringing a little bell beside a three-legged support stand with a pot for receiving money hanging down in the middle. Blake and the others left the car and began walking to the store.

Renaldo: That's a quaint little store. They sell boots and repair them as well, huh?

Jennifer: Yeah, it's my favorite place to buy shoes.

Blake: There must be some traffic through here if it's a good enough place for the Salvation Army folks.

Jennifer: The next store over is a Salvation Army Store.

Blake: Maybe that explains it.

Renaldo: You think they get many donations from their own customers? It makes sense to me. They're grateful for the discount, right?

Blake: Makes sense to me too. I actually like the Salvation Army. I think I'll make a donation.

Jennifer and Renaldo go on into the boot shop. Blake stops, takes out his wallet, and searches for money.

Salvation Army man: Hi, sir. Why do you like us? I just overheard you say you like us.

Blake: I had a professor in college who was a captain in the Salvation Army. He let me ride with him one Christmas break from Chicago to Louisville. He told me all about the Salvation Army. By the time the ride was over, I very much liked the Salvation Army. I was very impressed by their focus and interpretation of the mission of the church. It seems that they do more to help the poor and needy than probably any other church.

Salvation Army man: That's probably true, especially if you talk about what percentage of money taken in is given directly to taking care of needy people.

Blake: Yeah, that's what he said, and he had statistics to back it up. Before that trip I knew almost nothing about the church. In fact, I wasn't even aware that it was a church. Now I recognize it as one of the best churches. It's not very well known and it doesn't seem to have much status. It just goes quietly about the business of helping people.

Salvation Army man: Yes, it sometimes amazes me how little people know about us and how many people don't even know we're a church.

A lot of times people seem to think we're some kind of weird sect. They look down at us and even condemn us because of that. Many people don't seem to place any value on the fact that we do so much good. They're more interested in how much we're accepted by society or how much status we have. Because we work with poor people and we don't tend to have a lot of rich people in our membership, many people shun us and treat us with suspicion.

Blake: Yeah? Does that bother you? How do you deal with people looking down on you?

Salvation Army man: Well, it doesn't really bother me a lot. At least it doesn't keep me from doing the work and following through on my commitment, but I do think about it a lot. I always wonder how people can be so misguided and so callus.

Blake: Do you wonder if people think you have some ulterior motive or maybe you're a front for some criminal organization or something?

Salvation Army man: You know, there are quite a few stories of our people running into attitudes like that. I don't think it's widespread, but there are people who think that way. Of course, our country is full of people who hate people they don't know or understand.

Blake: Yeah, a lot of people think that if you're not like them then you're bad. Negativity and suspicion are very basic in humans and many times people hate entire categories of people. Often they're not aware of it. If you ask them if they hate those of a certain category, they will deny it. Yet hatred definitely shows up in how they act. Racial prejudice, prejudice against poor people, and suspicion toward certain ethnic groups is a well-known example.

Salvation Army man: Yes, and there are many who feel this way about poor people and those who don't have high paying jobs. They take the approach that poor people are poor because they are lazy and degenerate and that poor people don't deserve to be respected like others who are more conventionally acceptable. To them, the definition being poor means you're not to be respected as much as someone who has more status or is more "successful."

Blake: Of course, black people tend to have both of those things against them. They are obviously members of a race that white people shun and they tend to have a difficult problem with poverty.

But black people are not the only ones with these problems. In fact, most people have difficult experiences because of having things about them that others tease them about or say derogatory things about. Sometimes we exaggerate these weaknesses and frailties in our own minds. We forget that usually the criticizers exaggerate too.

Generally people are naturally oriented toward seeing negatives before they see positives. They tend to compare people in terms of who's better and who's worse and, of course, we're always favoring the idea that we ourselves have to be better.

Salvation Army man: Do you have this experience?

Blake: Yes, I've had it for various reasons all my life. When I was a kid, my ears were too big and they stuck out on the sides of my head. I was very self-conscious.

Now, these days, I belong to a little group that reads a book that claims to have been sent here by the universe rulers. Along with other things it claims that there are universe rulers. When the average guy on the street hears about this he tends to look at us like we're kooks. For instance, what do you think, do you think it sounds kooky?

Salvation Army man: Well, yes, it does sound a little kooky but *you* don't seem kooky. The real issue is whether it's true or not. Is there really a universe civilization and are there really universe rulers? If the whole idea is true and there really are universe rulers and a universe civilization, then it's not kooky. If it's not true then it IS kooky.

Blake: Yeah, that's the bottom line isn't it? Is it true or not? Unfortunately most of us are biased by our culture and think it can't be true. American culture has taught them that we humans are the only beings like us in the entire universe even though that's not really statistically reasonable when you think about it. It is commonly thought that the universe has only physical energy and doesn't contain beings equal to us.

Certainly American culture doesn't support the idea that there is an ancient government ruling the universe that is run by beings incredibly more intelligent than we are and far, far more spiritually developed.

Salvation Army man: Why do we know nothing about this? You would think we would have heard of it.

Blake: It is just now beginning to gradually dawn on us. We are actually a part of the universe system and they govern us now but they don't violate our freedom. They want us to realize they exist and willfully decide to participate in their government, so they stay hidden for now and wait for the right time in our growth and development.

Salvation Army man: That is a pretty far-out theory. No wonder it isn't very well known or accepted among our people. If our people heard about this they would think it's some alien group coming here to enslave us.

Blake: That's right. American culture teaches us to expect beings from the universe to be hostile and want to subjugate us just as we would if we were the ones with the upper hand.

What if I told you it's the same universe civilization that Jesus was talking about when He talked about The Kingdom of Heaven? We don't think of a universe civilization in Biblical terms. We think of it in secular, power-based terms. We "believe in" the afterlife told about in the Bible but it's not real to us.

I'm telling you about the universe civilization right now in real terms. Life as we will know it in the universe system after we die is real just like life is here is Earth. Death is just a gate and when we go through the gate and on into life there, we experience it as a continuation of this life here.

Salvation Army man: Well, it gets more interesting the more you tell me about it, particularly when you suggest that it is Jesus' Kingdom of Heaven. It actually sounds possible.

About this time, Jennifer and Renaldo come out of the boot shop.

Blake: Yes, I think it is true of this "theory" that the more you look at the details, the more possible it becomes.

Well, here are my friends so I guess I'll be going.

Jennifer and Renaldo exchange greetings with the Salvation Army man and he asks Blake for the name of the book. They both search around for a pen and some paper for Blake while Jennifer and Renaldo drift slowly down the street.

Blake writes the Urantia reference on the paper for his new friend as they say good-bye and he joins Jennifer and Renaldo. They also wave and the three of them move down the sidewalk in the general direction of Fifth Avenue.

Jennifer suggests they walk from there to Saks since it's only a few blocks away and it's unlikely they could find another parking place any better than the one they have.

Renaldo: Fine. I feel like a little walk. It's such a fine day. Oh, I hate walking on a big grate like this. It gives me the heebie jeebies.

Blake: And if you "step on a crack you break your momma's back," right? Remember that from grade school?

Renaldo: No. I think that one was before my time.

Jennifer: I've heard it before. Don't worry, Blake. You're not too ancient.

Fifty-Third Street was filled with trucks and cars, cars parked and double parked, and trucks making deliveries. Sometimes there was hardly a clear passage all the way from one block to another so a vehicle could actually pass through. It was a street very taken up with all kinds of business.

They came to the traffic light at Park Avenue and waited for their turn to cross. The Avenue was wider and more open here. Other people were waiting with them, quietly looking straight ahead, waiting to cross the Avenue. The light changed and off they all went. Our three kept walking down 53rd Street. They were continuing with their lighthearted chatter. All of a sudden Jennifer spoke.

Jennifer: Hey look at that, it's a FedEx store and I have that disk with me. Let's stop by there on the way back to the car and print out those questionnaires.

Blake: Yeah, it's great that we won't have to run an extra errand when we get back to the Lower East Side.

Jennifer: Yeah. I love it when things get easier, don't you?

Everyone smiled while continuing to talk and continuing to walk. They crossed Madison Avenue, went over to Fifth, took a left and they were at Saks in about a block.

Blake felt a tinge of elation as they walked through the brass-plated door of the store. Of course, he would never let it show through his poker face. As expected, they walked into colorful, well-tended elegance. The environment that closed around them was rich and well appointed with interesting draperies, glass display cases, beautiful figurines, and tasteful opulence everywhere.

Blake (in his private, inner self): I'll just ask someone if there's a section where they sell things only sold at this store. I'll say I'm looking for a gift.

Jennifer: I think the best place to go is the third floor.

Blake: Maybe I should ask that guy just to make sure.

Jennifer (looking a bit aggravated): Okay, go ask him.

Blake walked over to a counter and asked the person working there if there is a section where there are things only sold in this store. He was told to go up to the third floor and look around at the top of the escalator. He walked back to Jennifer and Renaldo.

Blake: You were right. Third floor. Where's the escalator?

Jennifer: Over this way, I think. Should I say I told you so?

Blake: Yes, you should say that. You were right and I should have just followed your lead. I don't blame you if you're mad at me.

Jennifer: That's all right Blake. I won't stay mad at you long.

Renaldo: You're not surprised that Jennifer knows her way around this place, are you?

Jennifer was the only one of the three who had been there before. Renaldo came to New York with his family when he was fourteen. Now he is twenty-eight but he has never been to Saks. He was as lost as Blake. Jennifer led them to the escalator and they stepped onto the little steel grate that became a step and rode up to the next level. Escalators were a novelty for Renaldo. He was enjoying their trip quite a bit.

When they come to the third floor, they walk out onto the floor and begin discussing.

Jennifer: What are you looking for?

Blake: Well, I'm thinking of a piece of jewelry but I have to be careful—Lacy has a fair amount of jewelry already. I don't want something that's just going to end up in the pile and lie there forever. I think she has a lot of necklaces and bracelets and I think they tend to be silver in color. I think it would be good to get something with color.

Jennifer: Maybe a pendant or a ring.

Blake: Let's go over here.

Blake wandered into a corner area where there were a lot of interesting objects. Very colorful, large, small, all sizes. There were wood carvings, porcelain figurines, tapestries, cloth covers, plaster statues, objects of plastic, and other interesting materials, elephants up on their hind legs, urns, vases, boxes, and art glass.

Renaldo went wandering on his own and Jennifer stuck with Blake in case she could help. Jennifer led Blake to an area of glass display cases and trays and stands of bracelets, necklaces, and rings.

He was talking with Jennifer when a nice looking lady walked up and said the magic words,

Saleslady: May I show you something?

Blake: I'm looking for a gift for my wife—a gift that is unique to this store.

Saleslady: Well, probably the most unique things are over here where we have quite a few very nice collectibles.

    She led them to a section that was just a few yards from where they had been standing. It, too, had display cases as well as boxes and trunks with urns and pieces of sculpture, silk draperies, tapestries, plates, and other attractive accent pieces—decorative crockery, and objects of art. There were silver and pewter kitchenware and many other lovely things to look at.

Saleslady: We have these beautiful Herend hand-painted porcelain pieces and figurines that are very unusual. I think they are gorgeous. You might also be interested in some of our Jay Strongwater hand-enameled pieces that are right over here.

    Blake and Jennifer began looking in a display case that contained Jay Strongwater handmade jewelry. Blake was very impressed by several pieces he liked. One was a beautiful hand enameled butterfly pin that he found particularly attractive.
    Jennifer called his attention to several different things and his wandering eye saw several other things. He liked a ring, a couple of bracelets, and a hand crafted porcelain box, but he kept coming back to the butterfly.
    After a period of consideration and discussion with Jennifer, who said Lacy would like the butterfly, he decided

to buy it. He beckoned to the saleslady who immediately came over. He said he wanted to buy the butterfly and she agreed that it was very beautiful and his wife would probably love it. She picked it up and started wrapping it and getting it ready for a box. She asked him how he would like to pay and he brought out his wallet and took out a credit card. The sales lady finished wrapping and putting it in a box, then took the card over to her cash register. In maybe a half a minute she came back and said the card had been declined.

Blake was shocked He couldn't think what to do, especially in front of Jennifer. They looked at each other. Jennifer raised her eyebrows and smiled. He took the card from the saleslady and looked at it. He has two cards from the same bank, each from different accounts. The cards look alike. He had put a red dot on one of the cards so he could tell the cards apart.

Blake (in his private, inner self): Damn. Why was that card rejected? It's the account with the money in it—the one without the red dot. Damn, I hate this.

He took out his wallet and couldn't think what else to do. He opened the wallet and there on the wall of the inside of the wallet he saw a red dot out of sight. He looked at the card and noticed a little smudge right about where the dot would be. Then it hit him what probably happened. The red dot had come off. He looked at the other card and it had no red dot. He knew that was the correct card—the one with the money. He started smiling and explained what happened. He gave the correct card to the saleslady and asked her if he could use his pin and make it a debit. She said yes, she could do that.

They went over to the cash register with the saleslady, she ran the card, Blake put in his pin and the transaction went through. Blake and Jennifer breathed a sigh of relief and started chuckling happily. The saleslady finished wrapping the butterfly. She put the little package in a box and put that box in another box with some literature. Then she gave it to Blake. He was very happy to have this important item off his list.

Jennifer: What do you say to having a little late lunch? I know a little cafe on the other side of Fifth Avenue that's pretty good. Are you hungry?

Blake: I wouldn't say I'm actually hungry but I could sit down and take the load off, have a cup of coffee with some drops, if they've got 'em.

Jennifer (lightly chuckling): I don't think they've have them. You mean you would actually buy someone else's coffee and their drops?

Blake: Just scouting out the competition, right?

They walked a little distance to pick up Renaldo and began making their way to the down escalators.

Renaldo: Mission accomplished?

Blake: Yeah, we picked out a beautiful butterfly pin. I'll show it to you when we get to the cafe. What do you say to going across the street and eating a bite at a little cafe Jennifer knows.

Renaldo: That sounds good to me. We could see what the effect of *their* coffee is. Maybe it'll make us really wake up.

Jennifer: Wait 'til you see the butterfly Blake bought. It's very beautiful.

They moved in a leisurely way toward the exit door, still looking quite happily at all of the beautiful items on display. They had been victorious in their quest. They had "climbed the mountain and obtained the precious stone." It was, of course, an American quest, a quest made easy by the owners. It was a quest attainable in America by anyone and everyone, who has the money.

As soon as they were outside, both Blake and Renaldo looked across Fifth Avenue to see if they could see the little cafe. It was easy to see. It had a large sign saying Cafe Gloria over the front windows.

Blake and Renaldo both asked: Is that it?

Jennifer: That's it. It's a very well-known cafe in some circles.

Renaldo: It looks like something out of Seinfeld.

Blake: Okay, well, come on, let's go over there. I feel a little like Seinfeld.

Jennifer: Okay, come on. I guess I have to be Elaine.

Renaldo: Okay, I guess Blake is Seinfeld. This is your show isn't it, Blake?

Blake: So who are you?

Renaldo: I don't know. I don't much feel like George. I guess I'll be Kramer.

Blake: Is this a show about nothing?

Laughter comes rolling out of Jennifer and Renaldo.

Jennifer: Today we're just pretending it's about nothing. But Blake's show is really about some of the most important business on Earth—universe business.

Renaldo and Blake look at Jennifer with big, surprised, affirmative smiles on their faces. Then all three look at each other with big, broad, knowing smiles as they start walking to the nearest traffic light to cross Fifth Avenue. It's one of those infrequent high intensity activities one does while just paying a lot of attention to what was going on in the environment and just keeping one's own counsel inside. There were, of course, lights and horns and people walking toward them as well as with them—a high traffic situation.

When they got to the other side, they went down the half block to the Cafe Gloria and entered.

The hostess immediately looked up and saw that they were smiling. She beamed a smile right back at them, particularly at Renaldo. He responded to her in kind, for she was beautiful. He immediately thought it was a wonderful moment and she, along with Jennifer and Blake, shared his private sentiment.

Renaldo: Hi, how are you?

Hostess: I'm fine and so are you, I notice (her face blushing a bit).

Renaldo: I surely agree. We'd like a table for three.

Hostess: You're three happy friends I see. I'll seat you right now. Please follow me.

She took them to a place in the back in a soft, quiet corner, calm but bright. As they walked Renaldo took a moment to chat with her. The sweet hostess felt friendly and warm and flattered. As they were seated, he gestured toward Jennifer and said she is an owner of a cafe too—the Starlight Cafe and Coffee Shop on the Lower East Side.

Hostess: Well, welcome to Midtown. What are you folks doing up our way?

Blake: I wanted to buy my wife a birthday gift from Saks.

Hostess: Oh, that's nice. Did you find anything?

Blake: Yes, we did very well (holding up his package).

Renaldo: Show us. You said you would when we got to the cafe.

Blake looked around at each of the faces and decided to open the package and show off the butterfly. Everyone was interested and quite impressed with its beauty. They passed it around making admiring sounds and the hostess went back to the front.

Jennifer to Renaldo: She's a nice girl and she likes you as much as you like her. We all felt the electricity. Of course Renaldo is pretty electrical with everyone, especially the girls.

Renaldo: Believe me, women don't like me as much as I like them.

Jennifer: Some of them do, don't you think?

Blake: I'd say probably so. Don't you sometimes get rushed by women?

Renaldo (smiling): Do girls do that?

Now the hostess returns with a woman who has a big smile on her face. The woman was well-dressed and attractive, exuding energy and enthusiasm.

Hostess (looking primarily at Jennifer): This is Gloria, our owner. I told her you are here and she wanted to meet you.

Gloria: Hello, hello (shaking Jennifer's hand). I have heard about the Starlight Cafe and Coffee Shop. I hear your coffee is something special. What's the ad say, "Try our special coffee. It helps you think." I need to come and taste that coffee.

Jennifer: Oh, hi. I'm so pleased to meet you. I hope you do come down and visit us. We would love to have you. Please say something to us when you come. I'm so excited to be talking with the owner! My husband has been in the coffee marketing business for a long time and we are featuring a new strain of coffee that was developed to have a terrific taste but be low in acidity. It is stimulating in a very positive way.

A waitress has approached their table now and Gloria begins talking to her telling everyone at the table about a couple of specials they have today. She also tells the waitress that the food for this threesome is compliments of the house today. She leaves and Renaldo, Jennifer, and Blake order some lunch.

Blake: That was a very impressive set of circumstances. It's clear that the word is out about you folks.

Jennifer: It really does seem to be, doesn't it?

Renaldo: Yeah, that's pretty exciting.

Blake: It's good we didn't tell her you're Elaine. We told her your real name.

Renaldo: I forgot all about Seinfeld when I saw the waitress. Besides, it's now the Jennifer show isn't it, now that we've met Gloria and realized that the Coffee Shop is a popular little place.

    Their food came and they started eating while they continued with the talk of the day. Blake had eaten half of his Reuben sandwich and all of his pickle when his cell phone began to vibrate.

Blake: Hello.

Caller: Hello, is this Dr. Blake Freeman?

Blake: Yes, it is.

Caller: Hello, Dr. Freeman, this is John Lane Billington. I'm the person you met on the train Wednesday. We were talking about Gurdjiefff and Ouspensky and The Copernican Error.

Blake: Yes, I remember. I was sorry after you left that I hadn't gotten your name. How are you doing?

Caller: I'm doing very well. I just wanted you to know as soon as I got to my computer on Wednesday that I looked up *The Urantia Book* and started reading. It was rather troubling in places, but I generally found myself very interested and excited. Yesterday I went out and bought the book and spent the entire day reading. I read a lot in the History of Urantia and in The Life of Jesus sections. As to the question of whether it's true or not, it seems much more likely that it's true than that it's some kind of hoax or trick.

Blake: Yes I've found most everyone who takes the time and gives it some honest attention agrees with you.

Caller: At this point I'm just getting more and more excited the more I read. I'm a full-time pastor of a small, independent, ecumenical church here in Reston, Virginia, and I feel that, with this book, I have found something catapulting me to an entirely new level of understanding and maturity in my ministry as well as my life in general. I've already found answers to questions that have bothered me for a long time. I feel a new level of strength and confidence that is transformative. It's profoundly changing my understanding of Jesus and Christianity. I think it's something I've been praying for a long time.

Blake: Wow! Those are pretty powerful statements. I know the book is quite capable of having that effect, though. What did you say your name is again?

Caller: My name is John Lane Billington but my mom always called me by my middle name, so people call me Lane, Lane Billington.

Blake (writing on a napkin): Well, Mr. Billington, I'm glad you called. I sure do want to hear your story.

Billington: That's actually another reason I called. I'm wondering if you are still in New York and if you're going to come near here on your way home sometime soon.

Blake: Yes, in fact, I AM still in New York and I'm planning to come home by train tomorrow.

Billington: Is it possible that you would be willing and able to stop here and stay over a little while? There's a train that comes through here from New York at 10:52 AM, and another one comes through at 1:14 PM. I could meet you there at the station and we could go to a little restaurant just down the street and have coffee or maybe some lunch.

Blake: How about giving me your phone number and letting me call you back later today after I call my wife and see what her plan is for tomorrow.

Billington: Yes, we can do it that way. Of course, I'll just wait until later this evening to receive your call.

Blake: That sounds good, Lane. Don't worry, I'll call you sometime in the early evening, after I talk with my wife.

Billington: Okay, take care then. I'll hear from you a little later.

Blake: Okay, good-bye.

Renaldo and Jennifer had been listening, of course, to half of this conversation and it had them both pretty curious. Blake told them the basic gist of the conversation—that the caller had heard about *The Urantia Book* from him and was very turned on about it. They were so full of questions, he had to go back over the whole story of what had happened on the train. They were very interested, especially when they heard he was a pastor.

Blake went over all of this and engaged with Jennifer and Renaldo in talking about it while they finished their lunch, stood, and walked out of Gloria's saying good-bye to the hostess on the way.

Back out on the street they started back up 5th Avenue toward 53rd Street. Along the way, they ran into a dog-walker with five dogs on leashes. They were stopped while one little dog deposited some poop on the little square bit of ground at the base of a small tree.

The dog walker stuck his hand in a plastic bag and picked up the poop when the little dog had finished. He put the "deposit" into a larger plastic bag he was carrying with his leash hand. Blake saw the strained look on his face and imagined he was saying words of complaint to himself about the little dog not being able to hold on until they got up to the park a couple of blocks further up.

They turned right on 53rd Street and headed east toward their car stopping by the FedEx store on their way to print out fifty copies of the questionnaire. They didn't make very many in case they needed to make changes. It read:

Starlight Café and Coffee Shop Questionnaire

Date _____

A recent popular theory says the universe is fully populated, organized, and governed by a central government.
What is your opinion? Do you agree?

_____ Yes, I believe it is true.
_____ It is possible and it probably is true.
_____ It is possible but probably is not true.
_____ No, I believe it is not true.

Is this your first visit the Starlight Café and Coffee Shop?
Yes _____ No _____
If No, how many times have you been here before? _____
Are you drinking the House Coffee with the drops added?
Yes _____ No _____
Have you had it before? _____
Do you drink it with food? _____
If Yes, how much food?
Snack _____ Meal _____

They each left the FedEx store with a copy of the questionnaire in their hand, walking slowly, perusing it. They soon agreed it would do for a starter and they would start getting responses from people tonight.

They came to their car, got in, and Jennifer drove the couple of blocks to Lexington Avenue. She turned right and started down Lexington Avenue toward the Bowery. She was beginning to get concerned that she would be late picking up Claire after school, so she called Mrs. Westerbrook, Veronica's mom, and asked her to hold Claire at her place until Jennifer got there. This was okay with Mrs. Westerbrook.

As they rode, they discussed the events of the day including the talk with the Salvation Army man, the gift shopping at Saks, the talk with Gloria, the phone call from John Lane Billington, and the questionnaire. Jennifer made a small joke about the job of the dog walker and his poop clean up, such a familiar function in so many jobs, including theirs.

Jennifer: Life is so filled with many kinds of poop.

They also discussed Blake's plans for tomorrow. Because of the meeting with Lane Billington, he had to leave earlier tomorrow. Jennifer figured she and Claire could take him to Grand Central Station in the morning in time to catch the train that arrives in Reston at 10:52. Since tomorrow is Saturday it should be no problem.

Soon they were back in the coffee shop neighborhood again. Jennifer did not go into the alley but stopped in front of the shop and let Blake and Renaldo out. She said she would go pick up Claire and come back to the shop.

Renaldo and Blake went into the shop and up to the counter and got a cup of coffee with some drops. It was mid-afternoon, and Raul, Monet, and Audrey were there drinking coffee and eating a few scones. Blake and Renaldo joined them. They gave a copy of the questionnaire to them.

Renaldo: Fill these out and you'll be our first responders.

Raul: What is it? Looks like it's mostly trying to find out about people who drink the coffee with the drops.

Audrey: Blake, are you trying to get some support for the idea that the coffee with the drops facilitates realization?

Blake: Yes, this is a first attempt to explore the topic.

Monet: Why are you asking about the universe thing?

Blake: Well, I think it's a good topic to see if people are realizing about because it's very singular in context, and we know it's a positive improvement of the established belief. This is not a concept people think about much and so it's easy to say they are realizing if they say they are favoring it being true because generally our whole culture starts with the idea that it's not true.

Audrey: Favoring it being true is a realization that it is at least slightly true.

Blake: Yes, you're right. You have to remember that I, more than anyone around here, know it's true so, for me, it works for the realization question.

Monet: Yeah, I see. Assuming it is true, it actually is a pretty good realization to be using.

Renaldo: How 'bout you guys? Are you thinking very much that the coffee facilitates realization?

Audrey: Actually, I think I am.

Raul: Me, too.

Monet: Of course, it makes sense that you would notice it most if it is facilitating realization right in the beginning, when you first start drinking the coffee. After you've been drinking it for a while, it's harder to actually say your realizations are connected to the coffee. The idea would be that after you've been drinking it for a while you're having realizations more all the time.

Blake: Yes, that's right. On this questionnaire we're going to be most interested in the people who have had the coffee for the first time.

Audrey: I feel as though I have generally increased my level of having realizations. I notice myself realizing things all the time these days.

Renaldo: What are some of the realizations you've been having?

Audrey: Well, something I've been really working on a lot these days is not overthinking things. I have a habit of just getting something on my mind and wearing it out. I just keep on thinking on it. I realize that I have to wake up to let something go.

Monet: One thing I'm seeing is that I always have an underlying agenda. I don't often just do something good for someone without an agenda.

Blake: That's a good one to work on.

Audrey: Another thing I've been noticing is that my feelings are not always as right as I have believed in the past. Especially negative feelings are usually something you *don't* want to believe in and follow.

During this conversation, Alicia and Robert come in and a couple of other regulars came in the door. They immediately get copies of the questionnaire and pick up on the conversation. At about this time, Jennifer came through the door that leads to the back and Claire is following her. Evan, Blake, and Renaldo are over on the side listening to the conversations and talking to one another. Blake is talking about leaving early in the morning and that the questionnaire looks good.

Jennifer walks over to the regulars' corner and quickly sees that they are talking about realizations. She raises her hand and speaks.

Jennifer: May I tell you about a realization that has been coming to me very strong?

All heads and eyes turn her way.

Jennifer: I've been realizing that The Urantia Book is far, far more likely to be true than not. I figure questions like these that are impossible to know about for sure and, by the way, *most* questions are like that. They have to be decided on the basis of probability. So, is The Urantia Book probably true or not true? Well, first of all, it overwhelmingly seems true on the face of it. It says nothing that is obviously not true. And it is filled with things that are positive, hopeful, logical, reasonable, and quite apparently true.

Secondly, if it's not true then what is it? Could any human or group of human beings make it all up and make it appear so true? Why would they do so and do so anonymously? If it is nothing but totally sinister and meant to foil and defeat us all, how likely is it to be successful at doing that? *If it is meant to distract us and lead us into an untrue path to prevent us from finding "the true path"? And if so, what is the true path it is trying to distract us from?* If we do find that true path, are we likely not to follow it because of The Urantia Book? I don't think so.

So, to me it seems far more likely to be true than to not be true and, if it is true, then it *is* what it says it is—the Fifth Epochal Revelation. If it is *true* and it is the Fifth Epochal

Revelation, then it is all the proof we need that the universe is populated, organized, and governed just as Blake says it is. The book tells us quite plainly and in considerable detail that space is not cold, dark, and empty. The Kingdom of Heaven is real and we can bring it to fruition on Earth by realizing the truth about it.

When Jennifer finished talking, there was a very short silence and then all the regulars present started clapping. Then they continued clapping and they started standing up. It was the only time in her life Jennifer had ever received a standing ovation.

People started talking about what Jennifer said. It obviously made a lot of sense to them. They were doing a lot of realizing. They shared with each other all of their various perspectives and insights. A very lively, positive, and up-beat conversation ensued that went on for several hours.

During that time Blake played a game of *Sorry* with Claire, listened, and talked with the regulars about the "realization questionnaire project" relative to the new coffee, and went out for a walk with Renaldo telling him good-bye for this trip, promising to see him again soon and encouraging him to stay in touch by phone and e-mail. Back at the shop, he ate a chicken salad sandwich and rode home to the apartment with Jennifer and Claire when Evan gave them all a ride.

When they got to the apartment and Jennifer put Claire to bed. Blake called Lacy to tell her the plan for the next day. He gave her the time his train would arrive in Union Station in Washington.

Then he and Jennifer talked a little bit, recapping all of the events of his visit and the issues they were engaging. Is The Urantia Book true or not? Is the universe populated, organized, and governed? Does the coffee facilitate realization? What are the various things they are doing to further realizations about the universe but also personal realizations that help people grow spiritually?

The next morning everyone was awake and moving at about the same time as the other days of the week. No sleeping-in this Saturday. In fact, there was a slight feeling of hurry because Blake had to be uptown at the train station at a specific time and they weren't sure how much time it would take to drive up there. Better be early than late.

Blake took a shower, ate a little cereal, packed up his backpack, made his bed, and checked around to be sure he was leaving the room the way he found it without leaving anything behind. Then they all went downstairs and Evan and Blake went to get the car. They said some good-byes on the way, complained about not having enough time to really visit, and made promises to keep going with the project.

After Jennifer and Claire got in the car with them, Evan went into a fairly extensive talk about his realization that finding out whether the coffee facilitates realization is not the only thing they are working on. They are also trying to foster the general realization in the public at large that the universe is populated, organized, and governed. He talked about how much he personally has come to see the importance of this issue, just since Blake's visit.

Evan, Jennifer, and Claire dropped Blake off at Grand Central Station. Blake said good-bye to each one of them personally and told them what a great trip it had been. Jennifer said she thinks her life is changed forever. Blake looked intently at his long-time friend and said, "Onward and Upward," an old farewell they had used years ago. He said he knew it wouldn't be long before they saw each other again and promised to follow up regularly on the realization project. Then he shouldered his backpack and walked into the train station.

When they first got to the station it seemed that they had arrived in good time but by the time he took care of his ticket and figured out where the train was, he barely got on the train and in a seat in one of the cars he liked to ride before the big steel car began to move. It wasn't long before he was pleased to see a familiar face coming down the aisle. It was Souther's week to work on Saturday.

Souther: Wow, I'm really lucky that today is my Saturday. If it isn't Dr. Blake Freeman. Have you been in New York ever since Wednesday, Doc?

Blake: Yeah, sure have. Of course, I don't know if this luck you're talking about is good luck or bad luck.

Souther: I guess you'll have to let me be the judge of that. I'm glad to see you. Did you get some good work done in New York?

Blake: You know, we really did and, most of all, it was work that I think is really important. So, I really like what we did.

Souther: That sounds great. What kind of things were you working on, if you don't mind my asking?

Blake: Well, let me ask you, Souther, do you think the universe is populated, organized, and governed?

Souther: Populated, organized, and governed. You mean do I think the universe has a lot of people in it and they are all arranged in groups or countries that have a government?

Blake: Yeah, basically that's what I'm asking.

Souther: Well, that's a kind of different way of saying it but I wouldn't be surprised if that's the way things are. I mean it's Heaven isn't it, and there *must* be an awful lot of people up there.

Blake: Yeah, and do you think the people who are up there are still basically the way they were when they were down here?

Souther: Well, maybe but I hope some of them are better. It seems like they would learn their lesson.

Blake: You think people get better up there?

Souther: I sure do hope so.

Blake: I hope so too and I think it's important to be serious about your hope.

Souther: Yeah, Doc, I think you're right about that. I think my life would be worthless without hope.

Blake: Yeah, that's right. Call me Blake. Let our friendship be what we both know it is.

Souther (looking Blake in the eye with a big smile on his face): That's right. That's right.

Blake: Listen, I just want you to be aware that I'm not riding this train all the way home today. I'm stopping in Reston to have lunch with a guy. Then I'm taking a later train the rest of the way home.

Souther: I'm glad you reminded me of that. Here, give me your ticket. I'll fix it so it all goes smooth today.

    Blake hands him his ticket. Mr. Souther makes a couple of notes on it and hands it back to him. He says he hopes Blake's day goes well and he'll see him later. He walks on down the aisle.
    Within two minutes Blake is asleep. He's had a fairly exhaustive visit with Evan and his family. His sleep is deep and relaxing. The next thing he is aware of is Mr. Souther waking him up telling him the train has stopped in Reston and it's time for him to get off the train.
    When Blake stepped off the train and looked to the left he saw no one he recognized. When he looked to his right the distance was farther and he did see a man down that way he thought might be John Lane Billington, so he started walking that way. After he had gone about fifty feet,

He heard someone call his name from the train station to his left. He turned his head and there was Billington walking toward him.

Billington: Hello, Dr. Freeman, good to see you again.

Blake (reaching to grasp his hand): Hello, it's good to see you. I'm glad you called. I was afraid I had lost track of you. I'm glad I gave you that card and I'm glad you called me.

Billington: I'm glad you gave me that card too, especially with the information that's on the back side of it. That information is a real game-changer.

Blake: And boy oh boy, do we need a game-changer!

Billington: Yes indeed. Ah, we're going to this little restaurant across the street from the station so let's go this way.

Lane Billington takes Blake back into the station through the door he came from. They walk across the large room that is the main hub of the station. Then they leave the station again on the other side through one of the front doors. They walk along the front of the building to the street. There's a traffic light nearby and they go there to cross. The restaurant is clearly visible.

They go in the restaurant and get seated at a table for two over on the side. Blake is studying Billington closely now. He sees him in a different light, as someone he wants to remember more.

Billington: Wow, that's really some book you turned me on to. When I stopped and really looked at it, I was completely surprised and amazed that something like that exists. It's pretty hard for me to understand and believe that I've never heard of it before. I mean, I'm a member of the clergy. I went to seminary and never heard of it.

Blake: That's a really good example of how people are asleep. We talked about that a few days ago when we first met on the train. People are very given to being asleep to things that are important in their lives. *The Urantia Book* is completely outside the boundaries of what people in today's Western culture believe about what's true or even possible in reality.
    And it's very important.
    It tells about what's really going on in the universe. Our people don't know what's really going on and most of them don't really want to know. They'd rather be asleep to the truth. It would frighten them and throw them very off balance to know the real truth.

Billington: I'm so glad you told me about it. During the last couple of days as I have been reading and thinking about the whole thing, I can almost palpably feel the organization of my mind changing.
    I told my friend David Leitnaker in Michigan about it too. He's been looking at it along with me. We must have had a dozen long-distance calls during the last couple of days. Both of us are really astonished.

Blake: Is he a minister too?

Billington: Yes he's my best friend. We went through seminary together. He pastors a church like mine in Michigan. We've both been saying we feel that we've stepped into true reality.

Blake: What's the name of your church?

Billington: We call our church The Resurrection Church. We very much like to focus on positive things and the future.

Blake: That's a good name. I like it.

Billington: I just keep thinking about your point of trying to help people see that the true structure of the universe really works to move us toward realizing the "Kingdom of Heaven" on Earth as Jesus wants us to.
    Our people are so oriented toward the outer physical world that if they could realize that the physical universe is fully populated, organized, and governed, they would be intensely nudged to grasp the Kingdom of Heaven as Jesus presented it.

Blake: It certainly would be a wonderful thing if even a fairly large minority of the people of Earth knew about the universe civilization and lived positively in the wisdom and hope that would give them.

Billington: Yes. Yes, boy, wouldn't that be something?!

The two men continued to talk and build their new friendship for more than an hour and a half until the time came when Blake had to get back across the street to catch his train. When that time came they both walked back across the street and through the station and out onto the boarding platform. They shook hands in a hearty, good feeling kind of way. They promised to stay in touch and each told the other not to hesitate to call.

Blake boarded the train then, with his pudgy backpack on his shoulder. He found a seat that looked good for sleeping, sat down and soon the big machine slowly began to roll toward Washington, steadily picking up speed as it moved out of Reston.

Chapter Seven

Norson

It's Friday morning and Blake has been to his office. He had an early eight o'clock appointment but that person didn't show. He also had two other cancellations this morning at 10:00 and 11:00. Nine o'clock was open and he always avoids scheduling appointments on Friday afternoon, saving it for paperwork. So he has a completely open day if he wants it. Even though the businessman in him is grumpy and worried about having such a day, he feels that childish lightheartedness he always feels when he has a cancellation or open time.

Blake (in his private, inner self): Boy, don't I love it when the work falls through. Lacy's not home. It'll be nice and relaxed there or maybe I'll just take a little ride.

He's driving on Randolph Road in suburban Maryland toward his house. He's looking forward to being there this morning because Lacy is busy in a meeting at the housing commission and he would have the house to himself. His mind is idling with lots of thoughts relevant and irrelevant running in a steady stream.

All of a sudden he finds himself turning onto Glenallen Avenue heading south. In the back of his mind he's plotting to take a little drive on a long way home. This is not unusual for Blake. He sort of believes in the great value of taking breaks and putting oneself in a position to be surprised by something interesting and/or enjoyable—a creative opportunity. It was the kind of spur-of-the-moment decision he does fairly often. He assumed it would be fine with his childish lightheartedness so it didn't worry him. He was thinking about Rock Creek Park, maybe finding his way over there. It's one of his favorite places. He drives through there often on his way from one place to another. It always gives him at least a bit of a feeling of peacefulness, even in a high traffic situation.

Peacefulness was rapidly increasing since it was Friday morning and everyone else was at work. It's not a high traffic time of day. He drove in a leisurely way around the gentle curves of Glenallen Avenue, letting peace and lightheartedness fill him.

Then a sign catches his eye that takes his mind away from Rock Creek Park. It's a sign with an arrow pointing to Brookside Gardens. He knew this place very well. He has been there many times but he hadn't been thinking about it. Now, all of a sudden, he is. He decides to turn in. He cuts his speed and makes a left turn into the parking lot of Brookside Gardens.

Blake (in his private, inner self): Let's go in. No reason not to. What a great place this is. I'm very much in a Brookside Gardens mood this morning. So help me, I can smell the increase in oxygen.

Blake got out of his car and locked it by force of habit. He walked through the familiar gate and chose one of the three paths that were presented to him—the one on the right. He likes that path and that section of the gardens. It has a little pond with some very colorful koi. It was early winter in suburban Maryland and the foliage on the trees and plants was minimal, but the garden layout was planned to include plants that present as much winter foliage as possible. It is as thick, attractive, and foliated as much as possible all year.

The path Blake walks along is quite private due to the way the ground is bermed, planted with holly bushes and conifers, and fairly thick with large trees having large trunks. An attractive swath of ground stretches on either side of the path but just ahead it's going up and over a little hill with some big rocks around the top. He follows the path up the hill and down into a small close draw, maybe fifteen to twenty feet wide running up some embankments on either side with little in it except the fine gravel path he's on. There is some grass on either side, a few thick, closely-cropped Nandina bushes, some small butternut trees, and some small boulders.

At the far end of the draw, just before the path begins climbing the next little hill, there is a fairly large, small boulder on the west side of the path. On it sat a strange character, otherworldly looking. Blake stopped with a soft gasp. Maybe it was an angel. It looked like a creature of light but very distinct. He or she was dressed in what seemed like an alabaster colored robe.

Ryndle: Hello, my name is Ryndle. I'm a secondary midwayer. I have been sent here by Norson to fetch you. He would like to have a meeting with you. He said you would understand.

Blake (in his private, inner self): A "secondary midwayer"? Hm, how does he know about secondary midwayers? Maybe it's because he is one. I need to consider that as a definite possibility.

Blake: Is Norson a Melchizedek?

Ryndle: Yes.

Blake: Then I do understand and I will come with you.

Ryndle: Okay, let's go over this next little hill. I have a means of transportation.

    Blake walks the twenty feet or so to where Ryndle stands and follows him up the sloping path to the top of the next hill where he sees something even more surprising and amazing. In front of them is a larger bowl of grass and landscaped views with healthy, thick bushes and small trees around the edges. Up the slopes of all the berms around the bowl and resting off to the side of the path in this pleasant and rich botanical scene, is a small ship about the size of a large pickup truck but very rounded. It is not rectangular or boxlike. It looks like a classic flying saucer, but oval in shape. It floats or hovers about three feet off the ground. It is very inviting. It is silver or metallic in color. It adds excitement to Blake's feeling of peacefulness.

Blake: Did you borrow this from the Disney studio?

Ryndle: Well, I guess you could say something like that—I *did* borrow it. Come on.

Blake: We're going to ride in this flying saucer? Or, is Norson in there?

Ryndle: We're going to fly to where Norson is.

Blake: Where is he?

Ryndle: He's in a big ship a bit off the surface.

Blake: Wow, off the surface, huh? That certainly has a ring to it. Sounds like fun. Can we do some joyriding, too?

Ryndle: I thought joyrides were things teenagers do in cars.

Blake: I'm sure they would do it in a spaceship if they had one; don't you think?

Ryndle: Yes, probably. Are you being a teenager today?

Blake: How do you get in this thing? (They had arrived at the little ship during their banter.)

One could say Blake was shocked into quite a state of excitement. Ryndle evoked an easy trust, especially after being told that the Melchizedek Norson wanted to meet with him. So now, as Ryndle noticed, Blake is rather like a giddy teenager with a thousand wild thoughts racing through his mind. All he can do is just "ride the river."

The little ship was floating about fifteen feet to the left of the path with what looked like its nose pointing out toward the path. Ryndle walked over to the right side and touched its side in a certain place. The ship rose about six feet and a large flap opened underneath. A ramp slid out at maybe a thirty-degree angle to the ground. Ryndle and Blake walk up the ramp and into the ship. Ryndle sits in what appears to be a "driver's seat" and motions for Blake to sit in the seat beside him. It's a seat that completely contains him; it is wrapped around him with what appears to be inflatable padding all around to keep him from bouncing or jostling. Ryndle explained that he should lean back against the back of the chair and keep his head back against the chair—at times they will be moving at high speeds.

Blake found his chair remarkably comfortable. It seemed to mold itself around him and actively grabbed him in a soft but uncompromising way. He yielded to what the chair seemed to require. Ryndle made no movements with his arms or legs. He seemed to be commanding the ship with his voice and possibly his thoughts, or maybe he isn't in command of the ship at all. The more Blake considered it, the more he thought Ryndle was merely a passenger, just as he was, and the ship is flying automatically.

After Ryndle said several things Blake didn't understand, some lights began to blink. There seemed to be some setting changes and there was a soft humming. The little ship began to lift up higher off the ground. When it got about twenty feet high, it begin to move off into the sky with an arching motion that threw Blake back into his chair and held him tight in one place. The humming seemed to get higher pitched and he felt some Gs, but he had the distinct feeling also that some mechanisms were at work to counter the intensity of the gravity pulling back.

There are no windows. The two riders couldn't see what things looked like outside the ship. Blake continued honing his theory that this is some kind of shuttlecraft and they are both just being ferried from "the surface" to the ship where Norson is.

He is mostly puzzled by the fact that Norson is in a space ship at all. That's the main thing that makes him doubtful about this trip. Why does Norson need a ship? It isn't exactly easy to tell how long they have been in flight, but it doesn't seem very long before the humming seemed to lower its pitch. Then there is some mild bumping that happened and the humming stops altogether.

Blake (in his private, inner self): Well, I guess we are here. I wonder what will happen now. I don't suppose there's going to be a film crew.

After waiting a moment, Ryndle said one of those incomprehensible words and the roof and whole upper section of the ship began to lift. It opened somewhat like a big clamshell so that right in front of the two riders, the side of the ship was just five or six inches above the floor of the room and room around them is just on the other side of the wall of the ship. Ryndle stood up and steps out of the ship.

Ryndle: Come on, follow me.

Blake: Okay.

He stood up, stepped out of the ship, and started following Ryndle. They walked along the side of the ship toward the back and down a long deck that passed about seven other similar little ships that were docked there.

The room was like a moderate size cavern-like room that did not have perpendicular walls. There was no other gear or furniture visible except what looked like some hatches on the wall opposite the ships. The room was big enough to house the little ships and perhaps accommodate any loading/unloading that might be done.

Their path led out of the larger room and into a hallway that sloped gradually up and curved to the left. They met no other people or beings on the path. Blake kidded himself about being the only ones there but he did not seriously entertain that possibility at all. Instead, he assumed that there were many others on the big ship. Perhaps they were even watching them as they walked down the hall.

Blake (after a little silence): I'd say that's a trip I'll probably remember.

Ryndle: Yes, and the main part hasn't even happened yet.

Blake: Yes, I know.

Blake (in his private, inner self): I wonder if it will really be Norson. I guess I'm playing my cards fairly close to my chest right now. Maybe I shouldn't have come here so quickly. I sure hope this doesn't turn out to be some kind of big hoax.

They came to an area where the floor leveled and a row of windows started on the wall on the same side as the docked ships. There were also doors on the other side of the hall. Blake stopped and looked out the window. Ryndle was fine about allowing it. Blake was very impressed. The view is exactly what he expected. This in itself was somewhat surprising to him. What he saw was a sky full of stars—vivid, clear, multitudinous, and beautiful. Down at the bottom where he could just barely see was the giant, dark arch of some heavenly body. Blake asked Ryndle what it was and he said it was the moon. Blake gazed on in silence for a while. Several times he sees some movements that he finds very interesting. Then he says, "let's go" and they walk on down the hall.

Not much further down the hall at this level, Ryndle came to a door that had a sign above it. There was a word on the sign written in some unfamiliar alphabet making a word Blake had no clue about. Ryndle knocked on the door and a response came from the inside of the room.

Ryndle opened the door and they walked in. It's as though they walked into someone's living room. Except for there being no windows, the room is furnished with a couple of couches, a couple of easy chairs, a coffee table, some end tables with lamps, paintings on the walls, and an oriental rug. Everything was well arranged and the room felt very comfortable.

Norson stood and walked over to meet them as they walked in. He patted Ryndle on the shoulder and shook hands with Blake.

Norson: Hello, Blake. I am Norson. Thanks for coming.

Blake: I'm very glad to be here and to meet you. It's been quite a surprising morning.

Ryndle: Watch out for Blake, Norson, he's a bit of a jokester.

Norson: Oh yeah? Maybe we can have him give us a comedy routine.

Blake: With all due respect, Norson, I have to say that I'm wondering what you're doing with this spaceship. You're not giving me a comedy routine are you?

Norson: Blake, I understand your asking that question. You don't think of me as using spaceships. I can see why you would wonder. This ship belongs to some friends of mine and they were kind enough to let me hold the meeting here.

I have several reasons for choosing this. First of all, Ryndle needs extra energy, a sort of special electrical charge, to be visible to you and it is easier to provide that on this ship and in the shuttle. I want Ryndle to be visible to you and I want him to be involved in our discussions.

A second reason for coming here is that I wanted to meet you in private and I can do that here with complete confidence. Another major reason for bringing you here is to capture your attention in a *big* way. The talk I want to have with you is very important and I cannot impress this upon you enough.

Blake: What do we need to talk about? I'm very curious.

Norson: I think the major point of concern for me is awakening. My group and I believe the people of Earth are on the brink of a great awakening. It has already begun.

Secondly, it is by no means early. It is something that is very much needed right now. We think there is something you can do to help this awakening along and so we decided to talk with you.

We have been watching what's going on with you and Evan and the coffee. We like your focus on realizations and on whether people believe the universe is populated, organized, and governed. Realizations are awakenings. We see that you are very motivated to help people realize that the universe is populated, organized, and governed and we would like to help you do something to stimulate a large number of people to realize that the real universe is very different from the way they assume it is.

Blake: I guess you have some ideas about how to do this and also some ways to help.

Norson: Yes, I believe so but we want to use your ideas as much as possible. We have faith that you have some very good ideas. We also want to know that you want to do this.

Blake: Norson, I don't think you need to worry about whether I want to do it. If we can come up with a plan that looks like it will work, I will put everything into it. Nothing could please me more than to work with you and make a significant contribution to the fostering of a major awakening on Earth.

Norson: I am so glad to hear you say that. It is what I thought you would say and it thrills me to hear it.

Blake: What are your ideas?

Norson: Generally, we believe awakening needs to happen in two major areas: the outer, physical arena and the inner, spiritual arena. We would like to see awakening in both of these arenas at the same time.

People on Earth today who believe in an afterlife don't tend to think that afterlife is lived in the same universe system Earth is in. So the afterlife they see is not *real*. They don't see that living on Earth and living in the afterlife all happen in the same sky. This prevents them from seeing the unity of God's creation. They don't think there is continuity between this life and the next life.

You are already talking about this with the people at the coffee shop. You're discussing whether people think the universe is civilized and governed. This belief does seem to be on the increase and we would like to help it along. Generally, people on Earth think of the universe as cold and empty and the few aliens who might live there are hostile and warlike—the way Earth people would be if they went to a foreign planet.

Awakening about the physical universe would help people unify their spiritual aspect with their physical aspect. This is very important. We would like to see people realize that the Kingdom of Heaven Jesus was talking about is the same kingdom of heaven you and the people in the coffee shop are talking about. It is real in the same way Earth and life on Earth is real. It is also the same universe talked about in The Urantia Book. It is a universe civilization that is real and alive and operating right now all of the time. Its government is actually already functioning on Earth and if the people of Earth were to awaken to this fact, their understanding of life and all of reality would undergo a magnificent improvement.

At the same time, it is important that people be awakened in the inner, spiritual arena. This would mean waking up and seeing the truth about what's going on inside of them in the personal, spiritual arena. People are healthiest when their spiritual part transcends their material part and becomes its master. People must see and learn not to go along with and pursue their jealousy and selfishness, their false pride and greed, and all the ways they are inclined to be self-centered. This is particularly true for those who see themselves as Christians and live as members of the Christian Church. Your focus on the "Copernican Error" is a good one.

Christians need to wake up to the truth about the many ways and times they feel negative about people in other Christian denominations or other world religions such as Islam, Buddhism, Hinduism, Judaism, and so on. It is important that they wake up to the way they really feel deep down about people who are not members of their group. It is important that they *realize* that all people of all colors are God's children and deserve to be respected, loved, and supported no matter what their nationality or financial position or socio-economic status or beliefs about reality.

They should wake up to the fact that their intense hostility toward various categories of people and their negative need to prove themselves better and gain power, prestige, and ascendancy over those with whom they are so much in competition, retards, obstructs, and prevents the positive development of their race and their planet. It will take time for *everyone* to have these realizations, but it would be good to get a trend going.

We have noticed that you already work a lot with your clients on a one-on-one basis to help them see that psychotherapy is actually about spiritual development, and spiritual development is a major purpose of life. It would be good for you to give them more details about what really happens inside of them when they grow spiritually so they can see more clearly.

Blake: What would some of these signs of spiritual growth be?

Norson: There are many things that indicate spiritual growth. After a person gets used to seeing some of them, he or she will be able to see more and more. Some of the things you could point out include:

- Spiritual development brings better bearing of responsibility, learning to carry on in the face of disappointment, and bearing up bravely when plans are thwarted or one's purposes seem at least temporarily defeated.
- Spiritual growth means learning to be fair and just, even in the face of injustice, adjusting ideals of spiritual living to the practical demands of life on Earth, and planning for the achievement of a higher

- more distant goal, while toiling for the attainment of nearer and immediate goals of necessity.
- Spiritual development involves acquiring the art of adjusting aspirations to the commonplace demands of the human situation, mastering the technique of using spiritual drive energy to motivate material achievement, living the heavenly life while continuing on with Earthly existence, and depending upon the ultimate guidance of God while guiding and directing ourselves and our brothers and sisters here on Earth.
- Often it means wresting victory from the very jaws of defeat and transforming the difficulties of time into the triumphs of eternity.

Blake: Yes, those are good. I can see how those things are evidence of spiritual maturity on the daily, personal level. Thank you for pointing them out. I understand what you're saying and I agree. Awakening is very important and it makes me happy to know that you and your group are thinking the time is right to try to stimulate an increased awakening. What would you like me to do?

Norson: We would like you to write a book. We think you could do that well. Our idea is to tell a story about both spiritual and physical awakening but really put the major focus on physical awakening since the people of Earth right now are so very oriented toward the material, physical world. This whole world is now very much wrapped up in addiction to materialism. It mostly started in America but the entire world is now following American and Western culture.

The people of Western culture are almost *completely* consumed by the outer physical world. They think it is *everything* and the *only* thing.

You could have the characters of your book know about and find out about The Urantia Book. That way people may wake up to the book in a more gradual and unfolding way. They would be waking up to the book as an explanation and proof of the physical universe civilization—the outer world reality of the universe kingdom.

Blake: That sounds like a great idea. In fact, there is a story about my friend Evan, his coffee and his Coffee House, that is unfolding right now in front of me. It's a "real life" story I could write about. I could talk about this coffee that seems to help people have realizations and the people in the Coffee House and their experiences. Their story could be the basic structure of the book. I can have the Coffee House characters focus in a big way on the realization that there REALLY IS a real universe civilization. You do mean for me to write a fictional book, right?

Norson: Yes, a fiction book about a non-fiction book that points to the true story that the highest authorities of the universe have commissioned an epic revelatory book containing much higher truth to be sent here to uplift and awaken the planet.

Blake: How exciting! I feel incredibly honored that you brought me here and are saying this to me today. It's a bit shocking. Why me? Why did you choose me to do this?

Norson: Well, we have been watching you. We know about the coffee shop and the coffee with the drops. We also know about your long years of reading The Urantia Book and your profound and extensive understanding of the information provided there. We also know about the other things you have written and your general orientation toward writing itself. We like what we've seen and we think you can do a good job with this. Ryndle, too, has been watching. He also likes you and thinks you can do a good job. We would like Ryndle to work with you on this project. He is pretty experienced in writing books in English since he was highly involved in the midwayer project that produced the fourth section of The Urantia Book. Indeed he was very instrumental in the initiative that resulted in The Urantia Book.

Blake looked at Ryndle. He saw his big smile and raised eyebrows. His esteem for Ryndle had just spiked up several notches as he heard that Ryndle had been involved in The Urantia Book project from the beginning. He knew that the midwayers wrote the part of the book that is a biography of Jesus and this writing had started the whole Urantia Book ball rolling.

Blake: So, what do you say, Ryndle?

Ryndyl: It all sounds great to me. I can't wait to get started.

Norson: We would like Ryndle to assist you with the writing of the book. He has said he is willing to make it a high priority. We would like the two of you to work together closely on the book. He can also be a liaison person between you and us. If you have any messages for us you can send them through Ryndle. We can also send messages to you through him.

Blake (looking at Ryndle again): So I'm going to be seeing more of you.

Ryndle: Yes, I guess so.

Blake's excitement about this was huge. He had been assuming without being aware that today's excursion was a one shot thing. Now he's hearing he's to have a continuing relationship with Ryndle (and Norson to a lesser degree). Privately he's almost beside himself with glee. It's hard for him to entirely maintain his poker face. He and Ryndle are both smiling real big at each other.

Blake (in his private, inner self): Boy! What a turn of events. I'm going to be doing a work project with a half-angel. I wonder how I'll get in touch with him or where we'll meet.

Norson: I can tell that the two of you will do well together. I'm sure you'll have no problem working out the mechanics of communicating and meeting.

Ryndle: Can we meet at your house?

Blake (in his private, inner self): Boy! I guess it'll be fine for us to do that. I don't THINK Lacy will have a problem. She tends to be a little more conventional than me and she's not a real avid UBK reader but she IS positive about it.

Blake: I certainly think so. I HOPE so. We'll have to see how my wife reacts but I think she'll be okay. How often do you think we'll meet?

Ryndle: Well, I don't know. It depends on how fast the writing goes. How shall we communicate that it's time to meet.

Blake: Well, I don't know that. How do you usually communicate with humans?

   Norson and Ryndle both burst into laughter.

Ryndle (still chuckling): Whenever I want to talk with you I could just remain invisible and come up and slap you on the forehead.

Blake: That sounds ok. I think I'll know what that means. Whenever I feel an unexplainable whack on the forehead, I'll know it's Ryndle.

Ryndle: Well, I guess that's okay even though I was just kidding. I could slap you on the forehead but of course I also could just whisper in your ear.

Blake: Okay, well, we can do either one. What will be a signal I can use to summon you?

Ryndle: How about something in your garage at home? I can get in there easy and I can just check it frequently. Let's say I'll check it at least every Friday morning.

Blake: Okay, I have a notepad on my workbench back in the back and I'll write your name on a page of it. When I want to meet with you I'll put that page up.

Ryndle: Okay, that should work fine.

They continue talking for a while getting their signals down and sharing ideas about the book. They are all three obviously very happy to have formed their new association and laid the groundwork for their new project. Norson makes some comments about the fortuitous quality of their successful meeting. Then at this point Blake looks at his watch (an older one that runs on its own internal works independent of the satellite). He immediately becomes a bit alarmed.

Blake: Wow, it's late. How long does it take to make the shuttle trip?

Ryndle: About four hours. Do we need to leave?

Blake: Well, Lacy has no idea where I am, and at this point it'll be around 8:00 by the time I get back. I hate to make her worry. My cell phone won't work from up here, will it?

Norson: No, not easily. Why don't we go ahead and end our meeting and the two of you can start back. I feel very good about what we've done here and I'm very much looking forward to our successful project.

The three of them embraced each other and shook hands. Blake and Ryndle exited the room and walked down the hall to where the shuttlecraft was docked. They were friendly and jovial as they walked along.

Blake (in his private, inner self): Wow, what a thing! I can't wait to get started. I can't believe that I get this opportunity. I will do whatever it takes to make a good book. I do *not* want to disappoint either Norson or Ryndle.

They arrived at the shuttlecraft. Ryndle opened it and they both take their seats. Ryndle is saying:

Ryndle: On the trip up here we went a bit slow, mostly to be sure to keep the trip safe and comfortable for you. We might be able to go a little faster on the way back. Just let me know by making this signal if you get uncomfortable.

He made a signal of holding out a flat hand and pushing down with it a few times. Blake made the signal with his hand to let him know he understood and can do the signal. The shuttlecraft closed and sealed itself. Blake knew no more about what was happening with it except he could hear the humming begin to slowly increase in pitch. Ryndle was saying words that are supposedly in charge of directing the ship, and the two of them were then in flight.

Blake (in his private, inner self): What an amazing little craft this is! What an amazing experience this little trip has been. I have some new non-human friends. Pretty wild! I feel *so* grateful and *so* humble that I get this chance. Never in all my life did I ever imagine my life would bring me here. It is such a far, far greater challenge and opportunity than I've ever had before. If the book is good and effective in accomplishing its purpose, it could have an incredibly valuable, positive, and powerful impact on the future of our planet. It's amazing. I can't fully process this experience yet.

Blake continued with these kinds of thoughts as he sailed through the sky on his way back home. He was a little uncomfortable about the fact that he knew Lacy was worrying. But he just kept telling himself her worry would soon be over and replaced by an even stronger and stranger story about his adventure today. The idea that they were going to begin to receive regular visitations from a bona fide midway character will really "scatter her chickens!"

It was now his place to worry about her and how she would receive the whole project, especially this new friend named Ryndle. Maybe she would see the potential of the project and be negative about them becoming involved so publicly in such a large controversy. He found himself telling himself he had his fingers crossed, hoping that she would relax and not get all upset.

Every so often Blake would look over at Ryndle. There he was real in his chair. He would usually return Blake's gaze, at least a bit. For long periods Blake rode with his eyes closed and lost track of time. He felt a little strange at times. It was a feeling rather like nausea but he wasn't sure. He thought about going faster on this trip because he was late, but he didn't think the strange feelings were severe enough to give Ryndle the hand signal. They just kept on sailing and at times he thought they had been traveling for a very long time. Then other times it seemed just a little while ago that they had been talking with Norson. Other times he thought they would be landing soon in the meadow at Brookside Garden where his car was parked.

This turned out to be true. At one point and he could feel the craft settle to a stop. The humming had lowered its pitch to the lowest level and he could tell from the way Ryndle was moving that they were "home." The lower hatch began to open and soon the long ramp had extended all the way down to the ground. Ryndle was saying:

Ryndle: Well here we are. I'm not going to get out. I'm just going to let you out and then go on to my center place.

Blake: Okay, I guess it's time to say good-bye. I'll get started on this book immediately and send you a signal in the garage as soon as I have something for you. It sure has been a wonderful day for me and I'm *so* very glad to have made your acquaintance.

Ryndle: I am also very excited about the project and extremely glad to get to know you. It's a very unusual thing you know, for us to be associated like this. I will be the envy of my entire group. I will also check your garage every

Friday at the very least and I hope you will feel free to contact me for any reason.

Blake: Thanks for that. I may just give you a signal next Friday just to check to see if you're watching. Or I may just want to introduce you to my wife. Will that be okay?

Ryndle: Oh yes. Please do that. I will be very glad to meet her.

Blake: Farewell then. I'll see you soon. Thanks again for everything.

Blake walked down the ramp and off a little into the meadow to get clear of the ship. The ramp receded, the hatch closed, and the little ship began to lift straight up into the air, moving quickly faster as it went higher. Blake heard the hum but it became quickly too faint as the little ship streaked off into the night.

Blake (in his private, inner self): I want to watch him take off. He's gone. My, my. Better call Lacy. She's never going to believe this.

He took his phone out of his pocket and punched Lacy's number while slowly walking toward the front of the gardens. As he listened, her phone rang three times and then she answered.

Blake: Hello (as he kept walking toward the front).

Lacy: Hello! Where are you?

Blake: I'm at Brookside Gardens. You'll never believe my story. I think I'll wait until I get home before I even try to tell you.

Lacy: What are you doing at Brookside Gardens this time of night? Aren't they closed?

Blake (her question just hit him with a new concern he hadn't considered): This is where my ship came in. You won't believe it.

Lacy: Your ship? Oh, yeah I think it's going to have to be a pretty fine ship to explain this one.

But now Blake had a new concern about the Gardens being closed and the question came up in his mind about whether they had locked their gates. He began to walk faster while still talking jokingly with Lacy.

Lacy: And the big surprise you have for me was on this ship, right?

She was actually getting a little hopeful and interested at this point with this talk about a ship coming in. But all of a sudden Blake's feelings take a dive because he had arrived at the gate and found it closed and locked.

Blake (in his private, inner self): Oh no! Now Lacy was going to have to come and get him and he was going to have to leave his car here until morning.

Blake (the tenor of his voice changing drastically): Oh *no*! Now you're really going to not believe this and you're not going to like it.

Lacy: What? There's more surprise?

Blake: Yes, I'm afraid so. You're going to have to come over here and get me because I can't get my car out. The gate is locked.

Lacy: What? What have you been doing? You mean you've been somewhere else while you left your car at the Gardens and now you've come back and you can't get your car out?

Blake: Yes, that's exactly what has happened.

Lacy: Where have you been?

Blake: How about if you just come and get me and I'll explain it all to you on the way home.

Lacy: *Damn!* I don't exactly want to go out right now. How 'bout if I just leave you there and you can sleep in your car?

Blake: Lacy—

Lacy: Okay, okay. I'll be there in a little bit.

Blake: Thanks, I'll be here by the gate.

Lacy: Okay, 'bye.

Blake: 'Bye.

Blake (in his private, inner self): Damn she's pretty pissed. This is not a good atmosphere for telling her my story. I'll have to go slow and wait until she has digested the stuff about the spaceships before I talk with her about Ryndle visiting. Oh well, we'll just have to see how things go. Lacy can sometimes get stuck on some concern that upsets her and she can't see the forest for the trees.

There was one of those smaller big boulders by the gate of Brookside Gardens and Blake sat on it. The night was a little chilly and he gotten a jacket out of his car. It just happened to be there. It kept him from being too uncomfortable. He thought a lot about how things might go with Lacy and what he might say to her, but he finally just abandoned all of that and told himself to relax and deal with her in the way that comes up. After about ten or fifteen minutes she drove into the driveway of the Gardens.

Blake (opening Lacy's passenger door and getting in): Ask me again where I've been.

Lacy (stoically compliant): Where have you been?

Blake: I'm not absolutely sure, but I think I've been literally on the other side of the moon.

Then he began to tell her the story of his day. He told her about driving into Brookside Gardens on a whim. He told her about running into Ryndle who seemed to be waiting for him. He told her about the little shuttlecraft, the flight to the big ship, and meeting with Norson. He told her about the book they want him to write and how it relates to The Urantia Book.

Lacy just looked at him speechless, even after he stopped talking. She was not a person who resonated strongly to the UBK. She just gave nominal assent to the idea that it was true because Blake believed that and she believed he had studied the issue thoroughly. It never had meant a lot to her. She had never paid attention to the incredibly important implications of the book if it was true. She had not seen it as relevant to her personally. She had always seen it as something Blake was into.

Lacy was not clearly aware of this, but now, all of a sudden, she felt the incredible impact of the book on her personal life begin to come crashing through. She was caught completely off guard. She had not started driving the car but was sitting there looking at Blake with her mouth agape. She was completely dumbfounded. Finally she stammered something out.

Lacy: You are not high on hallucinogenic drugs, right? And you have not been taking any other drug? You are telling me this story *actually happened*?

Blake: What I'm telling you *truly* happened. I'm not lying, not joking, not trying to trick you in any way right now. Are you able to drive or should I drive?

Rather slowly, Lacy pulled herself together and put the car into motion. She turned around and began to pull out onto Glenallen Street where there is very little traffic at the moment. She was shaking her head and saying, mostly to herself, "amazing, absolutely amazing."

Blake had not yet mentioned to Lacy about the part of the plan that has Ryndle visiting him periodically at their house. He was reticent to bring this up right now. He thought that maybe it would be best to go a little slowly and let the part of the story that he had told her settle in a bit.

Blake: I know the whole thing is astonishing. I'm still absolutely astonished myself. You can't believe how excited I am, though, and how honored I feel that they have chosen me to do this. I don't know what makes them think I'm a good writer. Writing is really hard for me and I don't think I'm very good. I'm also incredibly humbled because if this thing turns out good, and it probably will, it will mean I've played a part in a very significant, positive effort for the good of our entire world.

Lacy: I don't know what to say. I'm just amazed. I can certainly see how you would be excited. And I guess I'm excited for you. I just have to get caught up, I guess. It's all so surprising and overwhelming. Give me a couple of days. I'll be okay.

They drove on toward their house and there was a period of silence between them. Lacy drove through the traffic and made all the turns and handled all the lights while all the time shaking her head, obviously processing the whole affair in her mind.

Lacy (in her private, inner self): Everyone else's husband screws up and has an affair or gets a raise or at best gets some big prestigious award. Mine gets contacted by a couple of angels and is picked to do a great service for the entire planet on some cosmic level. I can't believe it. I guess I should be proud but I just can't believe it. I don't even know what it means. I want to think Blake is lying to me but I know that's not happening. He'd have to be really crazy to come up with a lie like that and expect me to believe it. Nobody, not even Blake, could come up with a story like that if it were not true.

Blake (in his private, inner self): Wow. I wonder what she's going to do. She doesn't really even believe in The Urantia Book, not really. I can't wait to see where she comes down about it all. What's she going to say when I tell her about Ryndle visiting at the house? What's she going to say when I start putting in all this time writing? I hope she comes down positive and is able to open up to the incredible opportunity that's here and all the learning and all the realizations.

It isn't really very far from Blake and Lacy's house to Brookside Gardens. They finished the return trip home mostly in silence and pulled into the driveway.

Lacy: Well, are you tired?

Blake: Gosh, I don't even know. Now that I think about it I guess I am. I'm surely looking forward to hitting that bed.

Lacy: Oh, by the way, a man called you this evening from Reston, Virginia. He left his number and asked you to call him back. His name is Lane somebody.

Blake: Yeah, John Lane Billington. He's that guy I met on the train when I was going to New York last month. Remember? I stopped in at Reston and had lunch with him on the way back. I'll wait until tomorrow to call him. I'm not really up to calling him tonight.

Lacy: Yeah, I do remember him. That's who it was.

    They parked the car in the garage and walked into the house through a small breezeway. They spoke during their usual pre-bedtime rituals as they moved in the direction of getting into bed. Blake usually got into bed first and as he was doing that, Lacy spoke up from across the room.

Lacy: I hope one of those guys didn't forget something and have to come by here in the middle of the night to get it or tell you something. I sure don't want to be awakened from a sound sleep by some angel knocking on the door.

Blake: You mean you wouldn't invite him in for a cup of coffee?

Lacy: Huh, that's an idea, now isn't it? If he drank a cup of coffee, do you think the coffee would just run through him and back out on the floor?

Blake: Lacy, do you mean you don't know the answer to that question. Didn't you study angels in college?

Lacy: You mean Angels 101?

Blake: Yeah or Angels 201. I think it's a sophomore course, isn't it?

Lacy (after a short silence): You know I'm jealous, don't you? I mean how many other people do we know who have ridden in a spaceship with an angel? Anybody would be jealous.

They continued on in this joking vein for a fair amount of time. Blake was glad to see Lacy joking about it. He knew it meant she was adjusting to the whole thing and in a positive way. He thought it was a good time to mention Ryndle's visits to her.

Blake: You had better watch what you wish for because it might come true. I didn't mention it earlier because I was afraid to, but you probably will be meeting Ryndle.

Lacy: Yeah, what do you mean? Why were you afraid?

Blake: Well, I was afraid because I didn't want to shock you anymore, but a part of the book-writing plan is for Ryndle to be a consultant and help me write the book, so he's going to come here at various times to meet with me.

Lacy: What! Are you kidding me! You mean we're going to entertain him as a guest?

Blake: No. It's not going to be a dinner party or anything like that. We're going to be working together. But I'm sure you will meet him.

Lacy: Oh no! Wow! Well, is he able to make himself visible or will he be invisible all of the time?

Blake: It takes a special effort and energy but he is able to make himself visible and I'm sure he will do that, especially in the beginning.

Lacy: I surely hope so. It would be creepy to have some guy around talking with you but you can't see him.

Blake: Well, let's not get ahead of ourselves and make ourselves worry about something that might never happen. I'm sure Ryndle will treat you with great respect and sensitivity.

Lacy: You think I might get him to take me riding in his spaceship? Maybe he could take me to the store some Saturday so I can be seen by all of our neighbors getting out of the spaceship.

Blake laughed and gave her a little tickle in her side. She winces and scrunches herself up. Pretty soon both had fallen asleep safely at home in their own bed together.

Lacy sleeps a deep restive sleep throughout the night. She has what seems like a lot of dreams, or the kind that leave you feeling puzzled and slightly uneasy as though you don't understand and maybe you'll never really understand a dream again.

She woke up well after the sun was up and saw that Blake had already gone downstairs. She lay there in the warmth of the bed and of the sun streaming through the window.

The occurrences of yesterday and last night were in the very front of her memory of the previous day. It was as though they had never left her mind all night. Now that her awareness has picked them up again, her shocked amazement was also there.

She pondered all the details she knew about yesterday's drama and Blake's central role in it. She particularly thought about Ryndle visiting them, apparently quite often. It looked as though she would actually be getting to know him.

Her inner experience was swamped by a wide variety of feelings ranging from fear to pride to anticipation to jealousy and skepticism.

Lacy (in her private, inner self): How did we get ourselves involved in such a thing as this, she thought to herself? It's all coming out of Blake and his strong commitment to that Urantia Book.

Lacy was feeling so many things coming from so many directions. She felt completely confused and all tied up inside.

She was in no great hurry, but looked forward to going downstairs and seeing Blake, Lacy rolled over and sat on the side of the bed. She slipped her feet into the slippers that are there and stood up, beginning to move in the direction of the bedroom door. She had already heard Blake several times moving around downstairs.

Lacy (walking into the kitchen): Well, I wonder what little interesting adventure we might find ourselves taken up with today. Anybody for a trip to Mars?

Blake: I don't know if I want to fool around with Mars. They say it's all red and everything. And it's filled with MARTIANS! Sounds like a place to stay away from.

Lacy: Well, that's okay, you just stay here. I'll go by myself today.

Blake: How'd you sleep last night?

Lacy: I slept pretty well. I feel rested. I think I was a little afraid to wake up this morning. I didn't know whether the space goblins were going to be waiting to take me away.

Blake: Well, don't worry about the space goblins 'cause now we got some real space good guys to help us out.

Lacy: What if they turn out to be goblins in sheep's clothing?

Blake: Hey, that's a really great question. That's what you're afraid of, isn't it? I'm very glad you can express that. It's brilliant. That's a great way of saying what everyone on Earth is afraid of. That's why we're afraid of the UBK and that's why we're afraid of God and that's why we're afraid of the universe kingdom.

Lacy: Do you think we're afraid of God?

Blake: Yes, most people on Earth are afraid of God to one extent or another. For many of them, it's the reason they worship God or that's the reason they like God. They're afraid of what will happen to them if they don't. And for the atheists, they're *definitely* afraid of God—afraid of what they'll lose or what they'll have to do by way of obedience if He turns out to be real.

Lacy: Well, I was just joking about the space goblins.

Blake: I know you're just joking and I love your joking. You're so good at using joking to work on your inner issues. I'm glad you're doing the joking now. It means you're not really that afraid and you're working with this whole thing inside yourself—getting yourself settled and balanced and positive about it.

    Lacy looked at Blake and gave him a big smile. He knew just how to compliment her. She loved that about him.

He smiled back at her. He was betting she would rise to the occasion and adjust to this thing in a positive way. She was good at doing that. Now he could see that she was taking that approach to this book-writing thing and he felt a great love and admiration and gratitude toward her. She's his girl and he's *so* glad to have her.

They kept chatting together as they moved through the various stages of eating their bowls of cereal. The conversation turned to a talk about their boys and what's going on with them at school with their music and their sports and their friendships. They discussed how to handle Ryndle's visiting with the boys and they basically decide to keep Ryndle from them as long as possible and play the whole thing down when it finally does come out. They recognized that if the book was of any value, the boys would at least eventually learn about Ryndle and Norson. They would deal with that at the appropriate time.

Blake finished his cereal and went over to the sink to wash his bowl.

Blake: Where's that note you made with Lane's phone number in Reston? I think I'll call him now and see what he wants.

Lacy handed him a small pad of paper with the note on the top page. It says:

        John Lane Billington
        Reston, Virginia ~~ 703-856-7182

He picked up a cordless phone, sat on the couch, and dialed the number.

Blake (after Lane picks up the phone): Hello, Lane. This is Blake Freeman. Lacy said you called yesterday.

Lane: Yeah, hi Blake. Thanks for calling. How's it going?

Blake: Well, everything's pretty good here. Staying busy. How's your church?

Lane: The church is doing very good. We have around a hundred people now who are seriously interested in The Urantia Book. Those people meet together about once a week to read the book. Their average attendance is about twenty.

Blake: Has it caused any problems? Are any people negative about it?

Lane: Yes, there are those who don't like or believe in the book and they get grumpy sometimes. And we probably have lost three or four people because of it, but not very many. I never bring the book up specifically when I am speaking to the whole church or some smaller group. I just use concepts and sometimes facts from the book. Generally, when I do that, I find most of the people like what comes from the book, even those who are lukewarm to the book itself.

Blake: Yes, I too have found that approach is good. It's very interesting that you can talk to people in regular everyday conversations and use material from the book and they really like it. But if you mention the book, they start backpedaling.

Lane: Yes that is very interesting but generally people are accepting the book as a legitimate source and are actually personally embracing the book more and more in our church.

Blake: That's really something, isn't it? Is it having an effect organizationally?

Lane: I think there is less bickering and disagreement in general, but I'm not really sure of that—I may be just dreaming it up. But, listen, let me tell you why I called.

Blake: Okay.

Lane: There is another Resurrection Church in Northern Virginia where the pastor has embraced The Urantia Book. He's a good friend of mine and he and I have been discussing the whole thing pretty much. He has been relating to his members about it similarly to the way I've been doing, and a group of serious people has emerged in his church as well. They have started a reading group. So we all have decided to combine both groups on a Saturday next month on the fifteenth. I'm wondering if you can possibly come up and meet with us then.

Blake: Well, I don't know. I'll have to check my schedule and talk with Lacy about it, but it is something I would enjoy doing and I'll try to work it out. Right now, off the top of my head, I don't think I have anything planned. Hang on just a minute and I'll talk with Lacy and see what she thinks.

Blake placed the phone down and talked about the idea with Lacy. He also checked his calendar and she checked her calendar. After a couple of minutes of discussion they decided it would probably be okay to say yes. Blake went back to the phone and picked it up.

Blake: Hey Lane, are you there?

Lane: Yes I'm here, Blake. What do you think?

Blake: I think I can do it. Now, that's on the fifteenth of May right? Where and when?

Lane: There's a YMCA here that's not too far from the train. They have a nice meeting room that's about the right size. We've arranged to meet there for the entire day, so just tell us when your train arrives and when it leaves in the evening and we will arrange to pick you up and take you back. That will be no problem. We will also have plenty of food.

Blake: Well now, I'm very glad you said that about the food because I *do* love to eat! Seriously, it sounds like an enjoyable day and I'll be glad to meet all of you guys.

Lane: Yeah, everybody here will be very glad to meet you, too. I've told them a lot about you. I personally will also be glad to see you again and get caught up on what's happening.

Blake: Okay then, let's go ahead with this plan. I'll keep in touch with you and if anything comes up that causes a problem I'll let you know.

Lane: Okay, I'll stay in touch with you too. I'm really looking forward to the meeting. You take care of yourself.

Blake: You too, Lane. I'll see you next month, 'bye.

Chapter Eight

The Future

With my lover lying next to me.
Still my love is lost.
'Neath a sea of daily drudgery,
Where all my memories lie tossed.

And I stare into the mystery,
For a light to spark my thought,
And a voice comes back in harmony,
You're not dead, my boy, you're just caught.

Go on and play with the cards you're dealt,
No matter what you lost or how it felt,
And when your strength is gone,
And you can't go on, give up your doubt.

And let your pain cry out,
And let it help you to remember,
Remember to sur—

WHOOOA

Randy: Damn, buddy! Why don't 'cha just *run* over me!
    Damn big, fat, road hog, gas-guzzling farm truck! Favorite vehicles of the road bullies. If you don't get out of their way they just run you over.

The big king cab pickup truck with its mag wheels, macho muffler, oversized tires, running lights, and stainless steel tool box just zoomed on by even though the top of the hill it was climbing wasn't more than five hundred yards away and it was a two-lane road at dusk. Randy Freeman, in his brand new $200,000, 2038 hands-free-feet-free fully-automatic Ford Star Cruiser continued picking his guitar, working on his new song, confident his miracle car would keep him safe automatically, even if he took a nap.

He looked down at the paper he was writing on, there on the little table in the middle of his cab. He could see everything outside for 360 degrees around and above the car through the heavily tinted thick Plexiglas bubble that covered him; no one outside could see in. But he was primarily interested in this song. He put the guitar aside and picked up the pen again but flashing, pulsating blue lights immediately distracted him as he topped the hill.

The road bully in the pick-up truck was stopped on the side of the road just on the other side of where the road Randy was on intersects a big, wide boulevard at a traffic light. The light was green for Randy. The pick-up truck was on the side of the road just past the intersection. The police car with the blue lights was sitting behind him. Randy was glad he had his car's speed governor set at just four miles per hour above the speed limit. He knew he could get by with that. He wouldn't have to worry. Besides, his miracle car had already detected the blue lights on the side of the road and had cut his speed anyway.

Randy: Ha, ha, big fat road hog farm truck got caught. Awww, poor guy. Now he has to give the county government $150 or so for speeding faster than I. Ha, ha, ha. That won't teach ya, will it?

Randy sat up and rubber-necked to the right at the entire scene as his fancy car went by at a slow, respectful speed. Then, all of a sudden it hit him: The truck was sitting on the side of the property of a *very* large, modern-looking, ornate church that faced the boulevard but had a parking lot entrance from the road. Between the front of the church and the boulevard there is a big, well-lit sign. He instructed his car to pull over and stop, but the sign was too far away to see. So he told his car to go on up the road and find a place to turn around and come back and pull into the parking lot of the church so he could get a better look at the sign. He wanted to see if it said what he thought he saw.

Sure enough, when he got back to the parking lot and stopped right in front of the sign, he saw it clearly. It said "First Church of the Resurrection, John Lane Billington Jr. Pastor."

Randy was amazed and excited. There on the sign in front of this huge beautiful church on a road somewhere not very far west of Kansas City he saw very familiar names that had been seared into his memory from childhood.

The Church of the Resurrection... John Lane Billington... he knew these names. He knew John Lane Billington in some way. John Lane Billington is an old friend of his dad's and he is the founder, Randy thought, of The Church of the Resurrection. The pastor on the sign must be his son.

Randy (in his private, inner self): Am I supposed to know him or know *of* him? His name and the whole topic of The Resurrection Church bring up a lot of memories. I've heard my dad mention the Church a thousand times but I don't remember details. I should have paid more attention to my dad's stories.

There was something about Uncle Evan's coffee that made you have realizations. All the people in the church drank the coffee all the time or something. Sometimes my dad's stories seemed so full of bullshit. There was something about how they all needed the coffee to realize the universe was populated and governed. But, of course, all they needed to do was realize that meant the Urantia Book. And I think that's one of the things. People in The Resurrection Church *do* read the Urantia Book, I think.)

It was really quite clear. Why would people doubt the universe is populated and governed? That is so obvious. But I guess there are still a lot of people who do doubt it. I just thought dad's stories were a bit over the top sometimes.

Whoa, here come some guys. Maybe I should ask them about Lane Billington. I don't know. They can't see me in here. They don't know if there's somebody in here or not. They may wonder why I'm parked here in the middle of the parking lot.

Two men had come slowly out of the church and were standing on the sidewalk next to their own cars. They were talking to one another but Randy's car caught their attention. They were gawking at it. It was sitting out in the parking lot without fitting into any of the painted parking slots. Its nose was perpendicular to the sign and facing it, and the two men couldn't see into the car. The outer surface of its bubble top was made of a metallic, mirror-like material. The entire car was low and basically looked like an oval pancake-shaped thing with a bubble top that popped up from the back when it opened. It was actually larger than a pick-up truck but it didn't look that big because it was so low to the ground. It contained motors and batteries and a deceptively large amount of cargo space. It looked like a little spaceship on wheels.

One of the men started moving toward his car and got in. The other man slowly drifted closer and closer, somewhat circling the Star Cruiser to see it from various angles. Finally he walked up to the place where the driver's window would be on a conventional car and knocked loudly three times. Randy told his car to open. The bubble top popped up a bit at the back and the whole thing started lifting open like a big clamshell. The top was hinged in the front and acted like a big hatch so that when open, its bottom edge is ninety degrees from where it was when closed. Now the hatch top was sticking straight up into the air and Randy stood up inside. The man from the church exclaimed in surprise.

Billington: Randy Freeman! Is that you? What are you doing in our parking lot?

Randy: Are you John Billington?

Billington: I *am*. I am John Lane Billington Jr. I am the son of John Lane Billington and you are the son of Blake Freeman. I have been an avid fan of Ramblerock for years and I've always known that you are not only the famous lead singer of Ramblerock but you are also the younger son of my father's good friend Blake Freeman.

Randy: Well, *byyy damn*! Isn't that *something*! We finally meet! I've heard about you, too, many times! Is it true that you guys introduced the entire East Coast to the Urantia Book?

Billington: Well, I don't know about the *entire* East Coast, but my dad certainly introduced the Resurrection Church to The Urantia Book, and not only did the UBK spread like wildfire through the Resurrection Church, but Resurrection Churches spread like wildfire so that now there are more than five hundred of them around the country. They are all pretty tuned in to the UBK and your dad turned my dad on to the book in the first place.

Randy: Is that true? I didn't know that. My dad has a tendency to be a little modest about his achievements. He has a lot of stories, though—stories that I have always played down. Some of them always seemed wild and a bit unlikely to me. Of course, he's my dad. Guys always get their dads wrong don't they?

Billington: Maybe. I guess they do, but they also get them right, don't they? My dad always said you were a lot like your dad. He said your dad was a rock star with no band and no fame.

Why don't you come on down out of that fancy car?

On the side of the car, an opening had appeared and some stairs had unfolded. They are somewhat like a stile. About three steps led up from the inside of the car to the top of the rim of the body, then five or six steps led down the outside to the ground. Randy walked over this, still talking with John.

Randy: Did your dad actually say that about my dad?

Billington: Of course he did. You have to realize, my dad had the very highest respect and appreciation for your dad. Your dad introduced him to The Urantia Book and finding the UBK was the absolute most important thing that ever happened in his life. He saw it as the greatest source of positive change that had ever happened to him.

Randy: How long did it take him to realize the book was authentic?

Billington: He saw it immediately. He had already gone to school. He had been through seminary. He knew what the issues were. He knew how to tell if something was real and substantial. Christianity and religion had been his major focus his entire life.

They were standing in the parking lot of John Lane Billington's church and each was very involved in the conversation. As they talked, John simply gestured with his arm and hand for Randy to come with him and they started walking toward the church. The other man, who had been with John when they first came out, had said goodbye and had gone home.

Randy: Of course, I've had The Urantia Book all my life. I didn't read it when I was young. My parents just told me about it. They told me stories from it and what it had to say about various topics. And, of course, they told me about the physical universe it describes.

I didn't really start reading The Urantia Book until I went to college and even then the reading was slow until at one point I really got into it. One of the best things I did was to join a reading group where we got together and read the book every week. To this day I'm still not sure I've read the entire book, but I basically know what it says and I realize more and more what an incredibly tremendous light it is for our planet. Considering its information, it is sometimes shocking to see what people who reject the book or don't know about it think about God and the universe.

To me it's clear that The Urantia Book is exactly what it says it is. It is an official communication from the leaders of the universe civilization to our planet. It's a revelation sent here by the highest universe authorities to lead us positively and truthfully into the future and away from so many old primitive, superstitious errors about God and His creation that have been dogging us for thousands of years and are obstructing our progress more and more.

People say it's not Christian, but they only say that if they have not read it. If they read it, they see clearly that it is absolutely Christian. It contains a year-by-year biography of the life of Jesus, and it confirms all of the true, major tenets and teachings of Christianity.

Billington: My experience is very similar to yours, although maybe I've been more thorough in my reading and broader in my study. I think it's a great advantage to be raised with the book; but, I don't know, maybe not. Maybe finding the book on your own is a more powerful experience. Anyway, I think we're both very lucky having the dads we did. By the way, how is your dad?

Randy: Oh, he's fine; doing very well, considering. They're both fine—my dad and my mom. They've got each other and I make sure they have everything else they need. They still live in our old house in Kensington. Your dad is deceased, isn't he?

Billington: Yeah, but my mom's still living. She's in an assisted living place here in Kansas City, Kansas.

By this time they had come up to the door of the church. John unlocked it and they went in. John first took Randy into the sanctuary and turned on a few lights. Randy was amazed by the vastness and beauty of the place. He was used to large audiences and he could imagine this place filled with people. That would be quite a spectacle. He expressed appropriate awe of the room and congratulated John for his achievements. He tried out their pianos and their organ and the two of them made lighthearted comments about the amazing place.

Then they left the sanctuary and went to John's office. It was a large room—large enough to hold a meeting of a very large committee. There was a simple, not overbearing desk at one end, bookcases, tables, and straight chairs along the walls, and three large couches. There were also several comfortable easy chairs in different arrangements and a couple of wingbacks. The room was tastefully furnished. It was decorated in pleasing harmonious colors with a soft, lush carpet. Randy pronounced it a very nice room and sat in one of the comfortable easy chairs pretty close to the middle.

Randy: To me God is obvious. I mean, look, there's no way to prove God or be 100 percent sure so it's a matter of probability (and, of course that's true of everything). There are two possibilities: either yes He exists or no He doesn't. Which one is most probable? You look at the reality we've got. You see it is orderly, incredibly complex, and it all works on and on and on mysteriously, intelligently, amazingly and eternally. It never breaks down, though some humans may see it that way. Can you have a reality like this without some incredibly amazing intelligence being behind it? Whatever that intelligence is would be God, right? What's most likely? It's obviously far more likely that God exists than that He doesn't, hands down.

And the same kind of logic applies to the question of whether the universe is populated, organized, and governed. What's most probable? You and I and all the other UBK readers know that the universe is populated, organized, and governed from reading the book. The book is the proof that it is. But then, after we live with that a while and keep studying and learning and growing, we come to where we see, of course! Of course the universe is populated and governed. It's just what makes sense in a reality like this, made by this kind of God. The universe is made by God obviously and obviously a universe made by God would be populated, organized, and governed.

So now the universe becomes the proof that The Urantia Book is true because it told us about the whole thing to begin with. It told us in detail about a universe that is populated, organized, and governed . . . a full, elaborated civilization. The book is the proof of a developed universe and the developed universe is the proof of the book.

Billington: That was a wonderful speech. Maybe I should call it a sermon. Surely you won't mind if I use it in a sermon.

Randy: No, of course not. Just be sure and give me my royalties.

They both chuckled and John told Randy he received too many royalties already, judging by the car he was driving.

Billington: I think the great little speech you just gave is evidence that my dad was right—you and your dad are both cuts from the same cloth. I imagine that to be very much the kind of thing your dad might have said. Maybe you're both frustrated preachers.

Randy: Or maybe you guys are frustrated songwriters or psychologists. Who knows? I know I certainly feel frustrated a lot.

Billington: Well, I certainly am glad to meet you. I'm a little surprised and maybe a little miffed that we haven't met before now. I don't think I can accurately tell you how much of a presence your dad always was in my family when I was growing up. My dad made many references to things your dad taught and he referred to many of them repeatedly throughout the years.

He also encouraged me quite a few times to read your dad's book. I finally did that when I was a junior in high school and was first beginning to look deeply into The Urantia Book.

I'm telling you, your dad's name was a frequently heard name in my home when I was growing up. I don't know if I should say that the stuff my dad said to me came from your dad, probably not. I guess it really came from my dad, but it just seemed as though your dad always had something to say about it that was very quotable. I guess we could say a lot of the stuff my dad told me came from both of them but it was very true and important and powerful stuff.

Randy: Well, you sure have stirred up my curiosity. What is this stuff?

Billington: There are several things in particular but I think the most salient thing I remember my dad ascribing to your dad was the idea of The Copernican Error.

The Copernican Error is the basic mistake all people make in believing they are the center of everything. And on Earth it is the mistake—aided by our history and culture—that makes us all believe space is cold, dark, and empty. We basically want to think we're the only entities in space, even though we know it's not true

The Copernican Error is the general error the public made in the times of Copernicus when they thought the Earth was the center of the heavenly system. They thought the Sun circled the Earth, not that the Earth circled the Sun. Each one of them personally also thought, of course, that they were the center of their personal worlds. All people have this error built in and it is the basic source of all the other errors that create our personal, psychological problems.

Your dad said, "Context is everything." By context he meant all of our values and beliefs that rule us in the back of our mind. A part of this context is what we believe about the universe out in space. If we think space is empty, we experience a very different influence than the way we are influenced if we think space is fully populated and civilized.

Here on Earth we are all still totally screwed up by the Copernican Error, both personally and cosmically. On the cosmic level we don't see or realize that the universe is populated, organized, and governed the way it truly is. And personally we all also have a very hard time seeing and controlling our selfishness. That comes from our Copernican Error. We believe we're right all the time and the way we see things is how they are or how they should be. Our attitude is constantly distorted by our overbearing, over-emphasis on our own self-importance—our basic selfishness.

As I recall, your dad said all real human problems, apart from medical problems, are psychological problems and all psychological problems are the result of error, and all basic errors stem from The Copernican Error.

Randy: That is *so* true. And you're right—my dad used to talk about The Copernican Error all the time. When I was a kid I got so sick of it. I would get mad at him every time he brought it up. But inside, within my private self, I always knew he was right. And, lo and behold, now that I'm an adult and on my own, it's one of my most important concepts. I actually have the brass to say it *is* one of my most important concepts because I truly believe my dad was right. People are deeply, selfish and learning to see it and not let it run and/or ruin your life is a *very* important thing. It is *very* important that everyone learn to combat, control, and overcome his or her Copernican error.

Billington: Yeah, I got pretty tired of hearing my dad talk about The Copernican Error, too. But as I grew older I was like you—I realized more and more how true it is. I think it's particularly good because it contains the idea that people are not just personally selfish, their groups are also selfish and they participate in that group selfishness. Of course, what our dads were saying is that our whole planet is selfishly involved in refusing to believe in the universe civilization because we're afraid we'll lose something important if we embrace what's real.

Randy: Yeah, that probably is what they were saying as a psychological explanation.

Listen John, what do you say to the idea of us going for a ride?

Billington: You mean in your fancy car?

Randy: Yeah, in my star cruiser.

Billington: Sure! I would love to go riding in your star cruiser. Where should we go and how long should we be gone?

Randy: I figure we could ride for about an hour because I have to go back into Kansas City to make a rehearsal by 11:00. We can leave all of that up to the car.

Billington: I need to call my wife and tell her know where I am and what we're doing. It'll only take a minute.

John picked up his phone and called his wife. He gave her a general explanation of what they were going to do and said he would be home in about an hour and a half. There was a bit of a pause and he answered saying, "Uh huh," and "Okay," at the end of the call. Finally he said, "Don't worry, I'll take care of the trash when I get home," and hung up. He and Randy left his office and went back out to the parking lot.

It was dark and Randy pushed a couple of buttons on his key ring. The car came alive, the lights came on, and the top went up. The stairs came down and the interior lights came on. The car was a hybrid electric car with a generator turned by a motor fueled with hydrogen; that part of it was very quiet. It emitted a soft high-pitched whine that could not be heard unless you were close.

Randy and John climbed into the cruiser and sat down. Randy told it to close up and take them roughly in a closed circuit that would bring them back to the church in about an hour. With that, off they went.

It was a nice night. The stars were bright. The moon was close to full and the sky was filled with light. It could all be seen with surprising clarity through the dome of the cruiser. The car rolled out of the parking lot and onto the small two-lane road headed west again as earlier.

John was amazed at the smoothness of the ride. It felt like the wheels weren't touching the ground. He looked up through the dome at the night sky. The universe seemed so close, so vibrant and alive. He seems to be seeing it in greater detail than usual. Each little twinkle of a star, each soft cloud of light, each little spot of color or apparent grouping seemed to stand out more than usual.

Everything he knew about the universe made him feel so much a part of it, and he thought about his companion this evening. He, too, knew an accurate view of the universe and here they are taking a spin in this incredible car together for the first time. It probably wouldn't be the last— two second-generation UBK readers, each accurately knowing the organization and functioning of the universe that will become common knowledge among all the people of Earth in the not too distant future, just as people a few centuries ago came to know Copernicus' theories as fact.

Randy: You know, I was thinking about what you said regarding being miffed that we didn't meet each other earlier. I can see what you mean. I remember wondering about you as a kid and why our dads never did anything together that included the families. I think our moms did meet several times at dinner parties and conferences, but the kids were never in on those kinds of activities. I mean, I'm sure it was just an oversight. Our parents were all so busy all of the time and we didn't live close to each other, particularly when your family moved out here. But also it seems that they were always so overwhelmed with their own agenda that they didn't think much about our generation.

I'm really rather blown away by tonight. I never thought about possibly meeting you here, even though I know you live in the Kansas City area. I've enjoyed talking with you. I'm incredibly gratified by the things you said about my dad and the fact that he has been so important in your life and the life of your family.

I was just thinking about my dad and his stories right before I met you tonight and I guess I've always been a little hard on him. I'm incredibly glad to finally meet you. You've helped me get myself straightened out about my dad. You're really right—we should have known each other a long time, not just knowing *of* each other. So yea for us. I'm *very* glad to finally meet you, man.

Billington: Yes, thank you, Randy. I am incredibly glad to meet you, too. We need to figure out some ways to keep in touch with each other from now on. Looking into that sky tonight you could say it's "in the stars" for us to build a relationship that basically follows in the tradition of our fathers.

You know, our parents left us out of things for some reason back then when we were growing up, and then we all got out of high school and went to college and started becoming the "older generation" ourselves.

Now we meet tonight by some strange twist of fate and I'm really glad. I'd like for this to be a beginning for us and let us not do what our parents did. Let's take a vacation together sometime and bring our kids and families together so something that seems like such a natural friendship can be carried on properly. I wonder how many people in my family have read your dad's book. I bet it's more than just my dad and me.

Randy: That sounds right to me. You know, I've never read my dad's book. I read little parts of it here and there, but never the whole thing. I was, of course, told about it numerous times by my mom.

My mom told me about Ryndle, and Robert told me about him, but I never saw him. I think I heard him a couple of times in my dad's study. That was back when I was very young. He had a strange voice.

Billington: Did you know about him when you heard his voice?

Randy: I asked my mom and she said it was probably him. She had already told me about him. Pretty wild, huh? I thought about it a lot back in those days. It's a strange sensation to realize an angel is visiting in your house. My dad always called him a half angel.

Billington: Sounds like your dad. Ryndle was, is I guess, a secondary midwayer, right?

Randy: Yes, a secondary midwayer. Of course, I never knew what that was until long after he stopped coming. A lot of the time I found myself wondering if he might just drop in on me and see what I'm doing or hear what I'm saying but he never let himself be known. It's kind of eerie.

Billington: I was thinking about that, too. Are you sure he *completely* stopped coming? I wonder if he and your dad still carry on their relationship at all.

Randy: I wonder about that sometimes myself. I don't know.
    By the way, is there any way you and your wife can come to our concert tomorrow night? If you can, I can give you passes. I'd love for you guys to come.

Billington: Yeah, that'd be great. I think we can, but of course I'll have to check it with Karen, I can't just pop it on her.

    So John phoned home again and asked Karen, his wife, about their plans for Friday night. This time the conversation is more detailed and complicated. He told her about their chance meeting and the car. She had a lot of questions (responding and exclaiming about it all). She reminded him that they had a plan to go see a movie Friday night and she had asked friends of theirs to go. She didn't know yet if they would be coming along, but she wanted to see the movie. John said that they could see the movie on Saturday but she said she had to go to a swim meet with the kids on Saturday and she'll be too tired that night. Besides they went to this big banquet John wanted to go to last weekend so it's her turn to do what she wants.

He explained they would be the guests of Randy Freeman, the lead singer. She asked him if he was who Randy was with right now and John said yes. She recognized him as the son of Blake Freeman who had been such an influence in his life.

But she's unimpressed by the invitation to go to the concert for free. She said she doesn't like rock concerts. The call finally came to an end and John told Randy he had to turn down the invitation. Randy was very disappointed but said he understood and gave John a card with his telephone numbers, his e-mail address, and his website on it. They also agree to friend each other on Facebook.

Randy: Well, that's a drag that you can't come to the concert, but we'll do it some other time. This won't be my last time in Kansas City. In fact, now that we're more connected I might come here more than anybody expects.

Billington: That'd be great. I hope you do. Come some time when you're not working. Maybe bring your family. We'll do something together.

Randy: Yeah, I'd like that. It's a very great night, isn't it?

This dome has the ability to increase and decrease its tint and the top of the dome acts differently from the sides. Right now there's very little tint in the top of the dome and the stars are very visible.

Billington: That's amazing. What a car this is! Perfect for exactly what we're doing with it right now, huh? Great car to go riding in. Great way to relax and get away from the stress.

Randy: Yeah, I used it for that a lot. It's a *lot* more than just transportation, huh?

Billington: Yeah, I think so. I'd pretty much say that's an understatement.

Randy: Listen, let's go back to where you were saying your dad quoted my dad a lot when you were young. What else did he say that also came from my dad? What would you say was the most important thing my dad used to harp on according to your dad?

Billington: Well, certainly one of the major concepts for your dad was The Copernican Error—people's basic self-centeredness or selfishness. But then I think my dad would also say that a major notion for Blake Freeman was the idea of self-review.
    Self-review is about being ruthlessly honest with yourself—honest about your own problems and negativity. It's about seeing the things you don't want to admit—the things you're asleep to that make you negative toward other

people. We *must* learn to do this to develop our spiritual self and be spiritually healthy. Life is all about spiritual development.

Self-review means instead of focusing on someone else and their problems and weaknesses, look at yourself. See how you contribute to the problem. When you're negative toward someone else, there's always something there to see in yourself. It's time to see the error in *your* negativity.

Let me tell you a story my dad got from your dad. It's a story about a girl who, as a child, had a very strong fantasy about being a princess and the daughter of a king. Blake called her Abbie. As a child, she acted like a princess all the time and made up stories about everyone adoring her and treating her special and waiting on her and doing what she commanded.

Abbie's parents indulged her fantasies and encouraged her by calling her their "little princess." They told her stories and got her movies about princesses and bought many gifts for birthdays and Christmases that helped her dress up like a princess and imagine that she lived in a castle and had everything a princess would have. They always tried to buy her what she wanted.

She loved being a princess and with her parents' cooperation it became easier and easier to imagine herself in that role. She spent more and more time making up stories about being a princess in every different setting of her life, including going to the grocery store or to the park or riding in the car or visiting relatives or going to church.

When she grew older, of course, she stopped playing princess and acting out her fantasies but she didn't give them up. She kept them to herself but the fantasies continued to be strong and get stronger. They influenced her greatly as she made life decisions. They shaped her interests and ideas about how to approach various issues. She particularly followed her princess fantasies as she decided how to relate to males when it was time to start dating.

Abbie only wanted to date guys who would treat her like a princess and open doors for her and let her go first and carry heavy things for her and always let her decide where they went and what they did. This approach to dating was a philosophy that said men are generally inferior to women and women should pretty much always have their way. As she grew into adulthood, this presented problems because she could find few men who would go along with her.

She went through several unhappy struggles and heartaches because she could not get a relationship going with a man she could trust enough to be close and work out an understanding.

Finally she found a man she really loved. She was hopeful that he would fulfill her expectations and treat her like a princess, but after less than seven months of being together he realized he could not meet her expectations and ended the relationship. She was heartbroken. She felt betrayed and couldn't believe he was so selfish that he couldn't treat her the way women are supposed to be treated and be the kind of gentleman he should be.

Abbie became very depressed. She began to feel like giving up. She couldn't understand why her life was going this way. She began to isolate herself, not get her work done, and slack off on taking care of herself. Her mother began to be worried and suggested she see a psychotherapist. She began seeing Blake as a client.

When she first started seeing Blake, Abbie was a perfect client. She was pleasant and attentive, very charming. She kept good control of what she revealed to Blake, but she seemed very interested and sincere. She was very invested in looking good to Blake. It was quite awhile before he began to understand her princess complex and her problem with wanting men to treat her as a princess. He talked with her about the deep unconscious mind and how it motivates and shapes what we do.

He taught her all of the basic psychological principles and concepts that help people begin to understand how the development of the inner self works. He tried to help her see that the inner self determines how people are and how they act. Then, session by session, he began to be increasingly more direct in pointing out to her how competitive and negative she is, even though she always looks so nice and pleasant. He let her know that he could see how much she strives in most situations to be superior and better than everyone else, especially men.

At first she was shocked by this and she thought seriously about not coming to see Blake anymore since he had what she thought was such a derogatory and incorrect notion about her. Blake picked up on this and told her he could tell she was contemplating leaving therapy but that it was her mind tricking her and trying to tell her she was *not* competitive and negative the way Blake was saying. He said she should be careful and be sure she looks at herself carefully, deeply, slowly, and with a ruthless honesty before she put off working on herself and makes matters worse by quitting therapy.

He clearly and pointedly assured her that the things he was pointing out in her were not horrible things and other people who could see these things in her were not going to reject her in disgust. Instead, they were more likely to see her as a genuine human just like them. He made sure she heard him when he said being negative and competitive are normal and that everyone has this kind of material going on inside.

Your dad, Blake, thought everyone had to see their own tendency to be selfish, at least to a minimal extent and then learn to struggle against it. He saw this as necessary for basic psychological health.

He explained this to Abbie who, at first seemed not to see that she was self-centered at all. She seemed not to see that her dreams of being a princess had become far too serious in the back of her mind. She acted to be seen as a princess and be treated like a princess all the time. When people did not treat her that way, or do what she expected of them, she became angry and blamed them or felt persecuted, as though her life was in complete shambles and she was worthless or horrible and she could not go on. She seemed to never entertain the notion that she should change and admit her selfishness. Instead, she blamed everyone else around her and the circumstances of her life. She felt more and more mistreated and misunderstood, as though everybody hated her.

Abbie seemed to expect other people to see her as the center of everything, the same way she did. She was hopelessly competitive and could not keep from feeling she had to be better than everyone else. She was basically asleep to these things in her spiritual/emotional/motivational system, so she couldn't develop an understanding that helped her admit she had these problems and realize that it would be good to give up all the competitive negativity. This would bring her freedom and a sense of being with other people and connected to the world.

She could not see that life is *not* about competition and being better than others. She thought relating to the world that way was normal. She hung onto every little achievement and acquisition that she could use to bolster her belief in her own superiority. She never could bring herself to do the work of waking up and seeing that striving to be better than everyone else is *not* the way to pursue life. It leads to nothing but trouble and unhappiness.

Blake tried to show her how to see herself and be honest about how negative and unfriendly her way of doing things was. She would always say, "Oh, I see," and nod and tell him he was right and that's what she should do, but she never could actually do it on her own because she didn't really see. She didn't genuinely believe it was true. She just said she did to please Blake and get him off her back.

She kept hanging onto the competitive style and the little, momentary enjoyments she got when things seemed to go her way and she could feel better than others. She gave lip-service to what Blake was saying but when it actually came time to do it; she never could wake up and acknowledge the real truth at a time when she could act to change it.

One day, roughly a year after the man she loved so much had ended their relationship, Abbie was in Blake's office and she was particularly depressed and agitated. She talked in a desperate way and would go back and forth between being very angry and feeling very sad, thinking the man she loved so much could leave her when they had been so close.

Blake comforted her by saying he knew she was feeling rotten and he was concerned about that, so now it was important for them to see this situation as a time that can show her many valuable things about how she related to the man who jilted her—things that can be changed so as to bring great progress in her personal therapeutic work. "Now," he told her, "is an excellent opportunity to wake up and see things about yourself that can be changed to great benefit."

Abbie told him she knew he was right. She could see that she had been very controlling with her lover and, though she was only faintly aware of it, she had hoped he would always treat her like a princess. She was also beginning to realize that she had thought he was so enamored of her superiority that she was completely surprised when he ended it. Now as she looked back, she genuinely felt a great desire to change and to give up her silly princess fantasy. She was angry at herself for letting herself get so far into the princess mentality that she had made a mess of her life. She vowed she was going to change and leave all that silly stuff behind.

Blake responded in a very heavy-handed way. He told her he thought it very unlikely she would change from her competitive orientation and bring about a significant change that would really help. She had told him she would before, but she never seemed to remember the changes to make when the right time came. He did not think she was going to make a significant change right now because she did not really believe in a deep, sincere way that the non-competitive way—the positive way—is better.

The next week when Abbie came to Blake's office there was a relaxed, light, quiet air about her. She sat down in her usual place and began the opening small talk with the same air of happy, peaceful composure.

Blake: So, what's going on?

Abbie: I have a very interesting story to tell.

Billington: She told about going into a large department store at a mall earlier in the week. When she came to the glass door to enter there was a man on the other side of the door exiting. He opened the door and hesitated for a bit turning to his side and looking to his left.

Abbie thought the man was doing what men should do and was holding the door for her, so she confidently began walking through. As she got right on the threshold of the door, however, the realization came rushing in on her that he was not holding the door for her at all. He was opening the door and holding it open while he reached behind him to pull the wheelchair of his young daughter through the door.

She looked down at the face of the young girl while her dad was now waiting for Abbie to clear the doorway. The girl was sobbing and there was vomit in her lap. She had apparently gotten sick while they were in the store and her dad was taking her out to take care of her.

As Abbie stammered out a polite apology she heard the dad say to his daughter, "Don't worry, princess, we have clean clothes in the van."

Looking into the misshapen, embarrassed, very distraught face of the little girl in her wheelchair, a voice sounded immediately and automatically in Abbie's head.

"She's not a princess," it said.

Abbie was shocked to hear what she had just said to herself. Even though the voice sounded only inside her mind, she was embarrassed, disgusted, and dismayed to hear her own thought.

"How could I be that way?" she thought to herself. "Am I that heartless? Am I so cold and uncaring that I compete with a sick little girl in a wheelchair about who's the real princess?"

She was so devastated by her own inner thoughts that she completely stopped her fast-paced, purposeful walking and slowly went to a remote corner of the store floor where she found a lone chair and sat down. Her attention was completely absorbed in her inner thoughts and realizations. She experienced several flashbacks of earlier times in her life when she had been particularly selfish and obnoxious. She was embarrassed and intensely regretful when she remembered them.

She thought that Blake was right about her ridiculous princess complex. It was indeed hurting her spirit. It had made her anything but noble and someone to look up to. She really did not like the idea of being a princess right now. It was the first time ever in her life that she thought such a thing. In this moment she was seeing herself as silly and immature for hanging on so long to her princess complex.

As she sat there, her mind was flooded with thoughts about so many different ways she was negative on a daily basis. She was constantly criticizing various friends and acquaintances inside her head. She belittled people's clothes and hair. She called people stupid and pathetic. She really lambasted men who don't open doors or let her go first or who look at her in what she thinks of as lascivious ways.

It was a while before she pulled herself together and began to reenter the present moment and her original reason for coming into the store. At first she actually had a little difficulty remembering. For the rest of that evening and all the next day this experience kept coming into her mind. She realized that this was what Blake was talking about when he talked about "waking up."

Blake was fascinated by her story and he told her that yes indeed, that was what he meant by waking up. He told her she had experienced an excellent example of waking up. He told her not to think that the waking up was over. To the contrary, it had just begun. She would now have more and more experiences of seeing herself in a truly honest way.

The two of them then had a very interesting and intense discussion about what was involved in going forward. They talked about her typical patterns and that she needed to be mindful of them and catch herself in the act of doing these things and stop herself. They talked about her tendency to blame other people for things that go wrong for her and her habit of talking critically about people she competes with and devaluing them constantly. They talked about her spiritual development and that it had just taken a giant leap forward. Blake told her that it was important for her to let herself understand more and more about the difference between being negative and competitive on the one hand and being positive and loving and cooperative on the other.

Blake used this story many times later to talk with people about waking up and doing self-review. It is a story that illustrates clearly and fully what self-review is about and the way it works.

Self-review is mostly about waking up to the real truth about what's going on in the deep unconscious mind. What is revealed is often hard to admit or face, particularly when someone is new to the process. It involves making therapeutic use of "the ruthless truth."

Spiritual growth is always about looking honestly at ourselves and not the other guy. You can change your own errors and your own negativity and you are the only person you can actually help or change. You can change you—it is not possible for you to change the other guy. This is basically what the Bible records that Jesus said when He talked about looking at the log in your own eye, rather than focusing on the speck in someone else's eye.

The first step in self-review always involves overcoming the natural defensive human tendency to say not me. When there's a problem, the first thing people tend to do is say, Not me! Not me! I didn't do it. I didn't cause this problem—

- It's his fault over there!
- That woman over there did—
- It's because this happened.

- They don't allow—
- They haven't done—
- It wasn't me. It's not my fault!

Overcoming this tendency to say "not me" is always the first step in waking up. So the second step then is usually to say "It *is* me. I did this" or "I did that." It involves becoming much more comfortable with being wrong or making mistakes, not so comfortable that it becomes okay, but comfortable enough that it becomes easier to correct or change.

Your dad, of course, is a psychotherapist and he says all real human problems, apart from medical problems, are psychological problems and all psychological problems are wrapped in negativity and are the result of error. He says psychotherapy is a natural life process. Everybody does it. It's just like walking or talking or making friends. Everybody does it, but we have a tendency to do it not very well.

Psychotherapy is about developing our inner spiritual self. It involves changing negatives to positives and correcting errors. We all live by major errors that constantly make problems for us. They are organized in our unconscious or deep mind—the back of the mind.

In the back of our mind are the beliefs, values, and assumptions that determine who we are and how we respond to reality each moment. These are riddled with errors—usually errors of assumption.

We all experience reality directly in two major arenas: the outer physical world and the inner spiritual world. The outer world is the world of doing and the inner world is the world of being. Both of these worlds work together and go together. They can't be separated. But, the *inner spiritual self is meant to transcend* the outer physical experience and be a guide. The inner self can wake up, transcend, and see both the outer and the inner worlds *truthfully*. It can "enlighten" them—show them how to operate. This is the key process of psychotherapy.

According to your dad *and* my dad, this psychological process of waking up is the key to self-review. It is the way to see the truth for yourself, develop your spiritual self, and correct the errors of assumption in the back of your mind that create negativity and obstruct your spiritual growth.

If we are driven by errors of assumption that tell us it is impossible for the universe to be populated, organized, and governed, then we are also going to say that a book like The Urantia Book is impossible; therefore, we reject the book without even looking at it.

The process of psychotherapy and spiritual growth is about correcting errors and transforming negative emotional "stuff" to positive. Negative goes with being asleep and in error. Positive goes with error correction and the discovery of the truth.

We have to learn these skills. We must learn how to wake up and practice good psychotherapy. We learn this by developing our spirit. Spiritual development happens through the process of waking up and realizing what's really true. Then we bring ourselves into line with it by transforming negative to positive. We learn to have realizations and promote spiritual development by seeing clearly the quality of our inner motivational forces. Are they negative or positive?

When we are having a heated argument with someone, we think we're arguing about our point but we're not really arguing about our point. We're actually having a power struggle with this person. We're trying to beat them or "best" them. This is negative.

When we're talking critically to ourselves about somebody saying they are bad or inadequate or lazy or ugly or wrong, we're really just telling ourselves we're better than they are. This is negative.

We get negative about people all the time. We get negative about other drivers on the road. We get negative about our bosses. We get negative toward our spouses and children. We get negative about people in the street. We get negative about people in the store, people in the park, people in the news, people in other States, people in other cities or countries or other churches or other clubs.

A major condition to wake up to is our chauvinism. All forms of chauvinism are negative and there are thousands of them. We're chauvinistic about being the best athlete, scholar, best dressed, best parent, best Christian, best driver, fighter, singer, architect, best at understanding, best designer, joker, businessman, most successful. We think we're from the best city or state, member of the best race or ethnic background, richest, best looking, smartest, coolest, nicest, best liked, best trained, and so on.

Negative is always primarily about asserting that we're better than someone else. Negativity is always about me as the center of everything, being better than someone else on an emotional/spiritual level. Correcting this is the key to getting better, having realizations, and furthering our spiritual development. This brings true transformation.

Negative is anti-loving and anti-life. Positive is loving and hopeful. Negative is about selfishness and going along with your Copernican Error. Positive is about doing the best thing for everyone and bringing about the true, the good, and the beautiful. Usually negative involves being asleep and not seeing that you are perpetrating The Copernican Error. Negative is our chance to get better, our invitation to wake up and make positivity. *Your negativity is your opportunity.*

Waking up is about seeing. First, we must see (realize) that the negativity is there—that it exists. Then we must use our will to do the work of actually changing our feelings or our emotional being to positive, even though sometimes this is hard and slow going.

This is the process of self-review. It happens when the spiritual self wakes up, sees the truth, and transforms personal negativity to positivity.

Self-review is important for everyone. We can't live successfully without it. It is the key to psychotherapy, the key to waking up, the key to spiritual development, and the key to life! Spiritual development is what life is all about.

Being successful with our psychotherapy, really becoming ruthlessly honest, and slowly bringing ourselves into more and more genuine states of positivity is the happiest and most redeeming thing of all in life. It brings us to the supreme satisfaction of lovingly serving our fellow humans. It makes us love more and more with a high quality of love and it brings us to do more and more service for other people and the entire planet because we want to. Now we love and serve and are fully involved with life for positive reasons we've never known before. Nothing creates greater happiness! Nothing fulfills us more.

So working on our personal psychotherapy is one of the most important things for us to take care of in life. It's not something to ignore or think it will take care of itself. It's something for us all to wake up to and be very intentional about.

Randy: I remember Dad used to say that we all live in two basic systems: a power system and a love system. The power system is negative, competitive, defensive, protective, and ready to beat people in order to make progress. The love system is positive, cooperative, collaborative, open, and ready to join people and work together to make progress. Everyone's psychology is a combination of these two systems.

We are all motivated by our understanding of each of the systems and the way we have put them together, no matter how sensible or nonsensical. The love system is generally more inclusive and sees a higher, more accurate truth. The power system can be rough and competitive.

Psychotherapy aims at increasing our understanding and the degree to which we are motivated by the love system and decreasing the degree to which we are motivated by the power system, even though some use of the power system is usually necessary in this kind of world. It's important to get the power system right—not too much, not too little.

Generally negativity, arguing, competing, and needing to be better than the other person are all about power. In a power system, it doesn't matter if someone likes what's going on or agrees with it. Someone above you wields the power and everyone follows the rules. The process of spiritual development happens when someone buys into the system and its procedures in a positive way and seeks to help the entire system see the truth more fully and clearly, not just because he or she is being coerced.

Billington: Psychotherapy is about decreasing and weakening our involvement in the negative power system while we strengthen and increase our involvement in the love system.

Randy: Wow! This is very powerful stuff. If people learned this and understood it enough to use it in their life they would be very wise. The positive way is the loving way—the loving way and the "awake" way.

Twice tonight you have made me very proud of my dad, John. I knew these things about him, but when something happens like what has happened tonight, it wakes me up and I realize what a great guy my dad is. He has helped so many people in his life and it really means a lot to me. Your dad also helped a huge number of people in his life. He is basically the "father" of the Resurrection Church, and now look at all the Resurrection Churches there are.

And, of course, your dad raised you and I'm very impressed by how clear and genuine you've been about the whole business of growing up under the wing of a great man. You see him so clearly. You don't get all bent out of shape about him. You have great poise. You're on a very even keel.

Billington: I did get bent out of shape a bit when I was younger but not now. I really love him.

The two men continued to talk about all of these things as the cruiser transported them through the night, the countryside west of Kansas City, and the time allotted. It was an extremely enjoyable trip! In a way, they were reliving their childhood, this time as friends who know each other not just of each other. It was something they both had wanted even though they had been barely aware of it.

In a way, it was also a therapeutic reliving of their relationships with their fathers and each others' fathers—a reliving of the high dramas their fathers had generated and taken them through in earlier times. It included a working through of some issues and a clarification of the great triumphs and achievements associated with their fathers personally as well as with their families in the heavy times of their lives.

In another way it was an experience that quickened their vision of the future and their place in it. It stimulated their imagination of where to go and what might happen—what would be good to have happen and help happen. It was a night to remember for each of them and a time of the establishment of a new friendship that would be inspiring and enduring for all time to come.

Smoothly, lightly the cruiser moved through the night. The two new friends continued to talk about the things on their mind—truth, love, positivity, life, eternity, wholeness, and realization. They kept flashing on the reality and importance of the universe context and the beliefs about it that so powerfully shape the frameworks and cultural background of "little" people like they are and all of us. They feel a poignant stirring and a subtle underlying awakening in their sense of the fabric of the times.

Randy: What a mind-blowing thing it is to recognize the reality of "eternalness" and everything that pertains to it—God and eternity and the eternity of His work. In the real, practical influences of unconscious context on regular people the question of whether we really are eternal and what it means is very profound for the Average person. Some say no to eternity, but I wonder if they've actually thought it through. I think it's a question of probability like the one I spoke of about the existence of God and the authenticity of the UBK. God and His creation is either eternal or not. What's the probability? Whether you say yes or no, either way is equally mind-blowing. No is actually incomprehensible. If you say no, then you're stuck with the question of what is happening before God and after Him.

I think that deep in the backs of our minds, in our unconscious context, we all know that God, His creation, and each of us are eternal. To me it's far simpler and more sensible to say yes. God and His creation are eternal and if He is eternal then that explains a lot about the dynamics of the positive and negative aspects of His creation. Only love, positivity, truth, goodness, and beauty can continue eternally. Love continues, hate stops. Positive continues negative stops. Truth continues error quits. Goodness continues evil dies. Beauty continues ugliness ends. Life, love, truth, goodness, positivity, beauty, these things go forward eternally but not their negative counterparts.

Billington: Boy! You're really quite a thinker. After all the considerations you've led us through today it's hard to see how anyone could choose the negative or doubt decision about God or eternity or the UBK or the idea of a civilized universe. Basically, those who say no to the idea of a civilized universe are just saying, "Our science hasn't proven that it's true, therefore it's *not* true." What kind of sense does that make?

Randy: Hey, look up there. Is that the spire of your church?

Billington: Yep, there it is. I was just now realizing where we are when you said that. It's like getting back from a trip to Mars or something. We've been all over the place tonight.

Randy: Ain't it fun?

Billington: Yes, I've really enjoyed myself. Want to take another ride tomorrow night? Tomorrow maybe we can go to Venus, or maybe some real exotic place in Orion.

Randy: Okay, I'll be here tomorrow night at the same time. Could you maybe pack some sandwiches?

Billington: Reality sandwiches, right?

The cruiser was turning into the parking lot of John's church again. Without getting any other command it went back to roughly the same spot where it had been when Randy gave it the last command. The two men said their good-byes and Randy told the car to open so John could get out. When he's out on the asphalt parking lot he turns back to Randy.

Billington: Oh, by the way Randy, did your dad ever decide whether the coffee at Evan's shop really does facilitate realization?

Randy: He did do a lot of studies throughout quite a long period of time. I think the overall result did seem to indicate that people who drink the coffee with the drops have more realizations than those who don't. Of course, that doesn't conclusively prove anything, but it is rather interesting.

He also did several studies of the difference between those who embrace The Urantia Book and those who reject it. Those studies also seem to indicate that those who embrace the book have more realizations.

Billington: Well, that's pretty interesting!
I'll see you later, my friend. We'll keep in touch.

Randy: Let me just leave you with one question. What will life here on earth be like when most everyone realizes that the universe REALLY IS a civilization like the one the UBK describes?

Billington: That's a good one.

The cruiser closed up again like a big clam and the car started to move slowly toward the road it had been on before all of this happened.

www.ingramcontent.com/pod-product-compliance
Lightning Source LLC
Chambersburg PA
CBHW061634040426
42446CB00010B/1406